DEIRDRE KINAHAN

Deirdre Kinahan's other plays include *HALCYON DAYS* (Tall Tales/Solstice at Solstice Arts Centre and Dublin Theatre Festival, 2012); *BOGBOY* (Tall Tales/Solstice at Solstice Arts Centre and Project Arts Centre); *Salad Day* (Abbey Theatre); *Hue & Cry* (Bewley's Café Theatre/Tall Tales; Glasgow, Romania, Bulgaria, Paris and New York) and *Melody* (Tall Tales; Glasgow/national tour 2005–08).

Other Titles in this Series

Deirdre Kinahan

MOMENT

NICK HERN BOOKS

London
www.nickhernbooks.co.uk

A Nick Hern Book

MOMENT first published in Great Britain in 2011 as a paperback original by Nick Hern Books Limited, The Glasshouse, 49a Goldhawk Road, London W12 8QP, in association with Tall Tales Theatre Company

Reprinted 2012

Cover image: aka
Cover design: Ned Hoste, 2H

Typeset by Nick Hern Books, London
Printed in the UK by Mimeo Ltd, Huntingdon, Cambridgeshire PE29 6XX

A CIP catalogue record for this book is available from the British Library

ISBN 978 1 84842 152 3

MOMENT was first performed at the Solstice Arts Centre, Co. Meath, on the 12 November 2009. The production transferred to the Bush Theatre, London, on 25 February 2012. The cast was as follows:

NIAL LYNCH	Ronan Leahy
RUTH PIGEON	Rebecca O'Mara
NIAMH LYNCH	Maeve Fitzgerald
TERESA LYNCH	Deirdre Donnelly
CIARA BLAKE	Kate Nic Chonaonaigh
DAVE BLAKE	Karl Quinn
FIN WHITE	Will Joseph Irvine
HILARY KELLY	Aela O'Flynn

Director	David Horan
Set Designer	Maree Kearns
Lighting Designer	Moyra D'Arcy
Sound Designer	Alun Smyth

The Price of Violence

The impact of violence is rarely confined to the initial events experienced by its victims. The ramifications of an act that can take mere moments to perpetrate can linger and echo, can ripple through family groups, through friendships and through time. It will leave few loved ones untouched. For many, the act can leave a profound feeling of helplessness and a burning resentment for a wrong committed on a partner, a sibling, a parent – its scars are those of powerlessness, fear and anguish, but also a longing for justice and appeasement. In time, though, these scars can heal, for the lucky ones, the ones for whom justice can be 'seen to be done'. These victims can learn to overcome their ordeal and rebuild their lives; for them recovery and closure is possible.

What of the families of the perpetrators, however? How does a family cope with the crimes of its own children, its own siblings, its own parents? The impact on these groups can be just as devastating, just as profound – and possibly more cancerous because there are fewer perceivable routes to redemption.

How difficult can it be for a loved one to forgive, let alone understand, terrible acts committed by their own kin? What strategies can a family employ to overcome the violent failings of one of their own? How do these groups forgive? How do they live with the pain of a conflicted love? And how do they cope? In an environment where much of wider society may view them with suspicion and distain at best, many don't. They bury their feelings or run away from them, emotionally and physically. They live in the perpetual shadow of a malignant shame that they cannot shift and ultimately they break. So it is for these victims that the price of violence can be unimaginable.

This is the emotional landscape that Deirdre Kinahan has mined for her play *MOMENT*. Themes of violence, anger and helplessness abound and are projected onto a family in chronic denial and raw, searing pain. It all sounds positively high-operatic or Greek. But Kinahan is far too skilled a writer to give in to the heady temptations of hysterical melodrama or soap-opera glibness. As her previous play, *Hue & Cry*, proved so beautifully, she can situate big themes in small rooms and always speak truthfully. She is also very, very funny. In *MOMENT* she gives us one day in the life of a family in controlled crisis, a family walking the daily tightrope of a perfectly functional dysfunction, and into this delicate and volatile atmosphere she throws a returning prodigal. Soon the layers of hurt, mistrust and deceit unravel and the sins of the past come screaming home.

The real triumph of this piece, however, is in Kinahan's lightness of touch and her ability to bed her drama down in the almost mundane details of regular family life. Here ordinary actions, such as the preparing of tea, the setting of a table, or the small talk of a family meal, are laced with hidden drama and unspoken hurt. It is drama of a most personal kind and all the more believable for it.

This play gives us the portrait of a family, imprisoned by a crime committed in the distant past, who are struggling with inherited shame and responsibility. Where the perpetrator of the violence has served his sentence and moved on with his life, his family have been locked into a state of petrified incomprehension, a purgatory. Kinahan shows us that the pain of guilt by association can wreak havoc within the confines of the family unit, and no one is spared the pain of its savagery. For some the price of violence can be impossibly high.

Mark O'Halloran

for
Gary, Síobhra and Sadhbh
Xxx

Characters

NIAL LYNCH, *thirty, from Dublin*
RUTH PIGEON, *twenty-seven, from Chichester, England*
NIAMH LYNCH, *twenty-seven, from Dublin*
TERESA LYNCH, *sixty, from Dublin*
CIARA BLAKE, *twenty-five, from Dublin*
DAVE BLAKE, *thirty, from Dublin*
FIN WHITE, *twenty-nine, from Dublin*
HILARY KELLY, *twelve*

Chronology

This play takes place in September 2009.

The murder of Hilary Kelly took place in July 1995.

Nial Lynch spent five years in care/juvenile prison. He then spent six years in London, studying art for four.

At the time of the play, he has been living and working in Cork, Ireland, for three years.

Note on the Text

At the end of Act One, the characters' speech overlaps. The conversations in **bold** are the ones that the audience hear, the others drone on in the background.

This text went to press before the end of rehearsals and so may differ slightly from the play as performed.

ACT ONE

The kitchen of a house in Chapelizod, Dublin, 2009.

There is a blue back door, upstage right, facing the audience, and another door to the hall, downstage left.

The kitchen is empty. The back door opens and NIAMH *enters.* FIN *is behind her, she does not want him to come in.*

FIN	Any sign?
NIAMH	No, but I'm sure she's grand, thanks, Fin.
FIN	I never knew you were from Chapelizod, so close to the park.
NIAMH	Yeah? Right, well, thanks for dropping me over.
FIN	We used to play all our matches in the park...
NIAMH	Right.
FIN	On a Sunday morning.
NIAMH	Oh... well, great.
TERESA	(*Off.*) Ciara?
FIN	Ah, there you go!
TERESA	(*Off.*) Ciara, is that you?
NIAMH	No, it's me, Mam.
TERESA	(*Off.*) Ciara?
NIAMH	No, it's Niamh!
FIN	She sounds all right.
NIAMH	Yeah, she does, doesn't she, I'll just go on up to her.
FIN	What a great place to grow up, by the park.

NIAMH   I didn't grow up here.

FIN   No?

TERESA   (*Off.*) I'm just in the loo, love.

NIAMH   I grew up in Templeogue.

FIN   Oh, we used to play there too – Tymon Park.

NIAMH   (*With no real interest.*) Great!... (*Shouts up to* TERESA.) I'll just be up now, Mam.

FIN   Another great spot for kids.

NIAMH   Not really.

FIN   Oh…

NIAMH   I'll have to go now, Fin, thanks.

FIN   Would you like me to wait?

NIAMH   No, it's fine, she's obviously fine, I'll just stay and have the chat.

FIN   You sure?

NIAMH   Yes.

FIN   Coz I can wait…

NIAMH   No.

FIN   Oh, okay.

NIAMH   I'm sorry, I'm just a bit tense… I worry about her –

TERESA   (*Off.*) I'm just there, love –

Toilet flushes.

NIAMH   I'll see you back at the office.

FIN   Oh, okay, Niamh, if you're sure you're okay.

NIAMH   Perfect thanks, Fin, see ya.

FIN   Right.

*She gives him back his scooter helmet. He takes
the scooter helmet she's been proffering and goes
to kiss her. She is awkward but she takes the kiss.
He hovers.*

I can come back in an hour or so and give you a
lift if you like.

NIAMH   No, I'm fine, it's fine, I'll see you later.

*She closes the door. She stands with her back
against it.*

Jesus.

TERESA *enters.*

TERESA   Niamh…

NIAMH   Hi, Mam.

TERESA   I thought you were Ciara.

NIAMH   I know.

TERESA   I was in the loo.

NIAMH   I know that too.

TERESA   What's wrong?

Is there something wrong?

NIAMH   No.

No.

Nothing.

TERESA   Oh?

NIAMH   It's just I was ringing the house all morning.

TERESA   Were you?

NIAMH   Yes.

Where is the phone?

TERESA   The phone?

NIAMH	Yes.
TERESA	It's right there.
	But why aren't you in work, love?
NIAMH	Because I was ringing and you didn't answer.
TERESA	I was in Tesco.
NIAMH	You were in Tesco?
TERESA	Yes, for the quiche.
NIAMH	What quiche?
TERESA	Have you ever cooked one of these?
	I really think I should just have done the home-made, they seem awfully small… Don't they look so much bigger on the box?
NIAMH	Mam!
TERESA	What is it, love, I'm trying to prepare tea.
NIAMH	Tea?
TERESA	Yes, tea.
NIAMH	At eleven o'clock in the morning?
TERESA	Well, Ciara said to cook the quiche early and let it cool. It's less pressured.
NIAMH	But what's the pressure?
TERESA	I think she's right, I'll do the second one as well, there's ham on it.
NIAMH	Mam, I was worried, you should have answered the phone.
TERESA	I wasn't here, I took a taxi to Tesco.
NIAMH	Well, why didn't you take your mobile with you?
TERESA	You know I don't like the mobile.
NIAMH	I bought you the mobile.

TERESA   Oh, yes.

         Well… will I put the kettle on, love, or are you not
         staying?

         NIAMH *sighs*.

NIAMH   I'll do it.

         I'll put the kettle on.

TERESA   Oh, good girl, Niamh.

         Lifting the quiche.

         And do you know how to manage one of these?

NIAMH   Here, show me.

TERESA   You're a treasure. I just can't make head nor tail of
         these convenience foods.

NIAMH   But why…

TERESA   And it's so nice to see you. I so rarely see you.

NIAMH   Please, Mam, don't start –

TERESA   Well, it's just that it's a nice surprise, that's all.

NIAMH   Is it?

TERESA   Of course… so long as you're sure that they won't
         mind in work?

NIAMH   Mind what?

TERESA   Mind your being here?

         You need to settle in this job, Niamh.

NIAMH   I am settled.

TERESA   Stay longer than six months.

NIAMH   Oh, for God's sake! And you wonder why I never
         come over?

         Silence.

TERESA	We'll have our tea.
NIAMH	Yeah.

Slight pause.

NIAMH, *having put the quiche in the oven, now brings over two mugs of tea.*

TERESA	You know I don't like to be a worry to you.
NIAMH	I know.
TERESA	You'll have to forgive me if I'm a worry to you.
NIAMH	Right.
TERESA	Because I know you have to live your own life.
NIAMH	Right. Grand, Mam, it's grand.

Another pause as they drink their tea.

TERESA	Well, your hair is nice.
NIAMH	Oh! Thanks.
TERESA	You got your roots done.
NIAMH	Yeah.

Slight pause.

TERESA	So you must have plans for the weekend?
NIAMH	Kind of…
TERESA	Really?
NIAMH	Well, actually I need to stay.
TERESA	Stay here?
NIAMH	Yes.
	That's why I was ringing, you see, they're doing a plumbing job at the flat and it's a mess…
TERESA	Oh.
NIAMH	Is that all right?

TERESA   Oh!

Oh yes.

NIAMH   Are you sure?

TERESA   Yes. Of course, it's just…

NIAMH   What?

TERESA   Well, it's just that… someone might be staying.

NIAMH   Staying here?

Who?

TERESA   Well… your brother is coming…

NIAMH   Nial!

TERESA   Yes.

He has to catch a flight early in the morning.

NIAMH   Nial?

TERESA   Yes, for a holiday.

NIAMH   Oh.

Pause.

TERESA   But you can always stay as well, Niamh – in the back room?

NIAMH   Right.

TERESA   I can make up the bed.

NIAMH   Right.

Pause.

So when did you hear from Nial?

TERESA   On Tuesday I think… yes, it was, it was Tuesday.

NIAMH   Tuesday just gone?

TERESA   Yes.

NIAMH   Okay.

You never said?

TERESA   Well, I haven't seen you, have I, love.

NIAMH   I suppose not.

TERESA   Would you like something with that tea?

NIAMH   No thanks.

TERESA   There's fruit shortcake.

NIAMH   So what's the news with Nial?

TERESA   And scones.

NIAMH   Where's he going?

TERESA   What's that?

NIAMH   Where's he going? Where's he flying to? Nial.

TERESA   Oh Lord, I can't remember – Spain I think.

NIAMH   Nice.

TERESA   Yes… and he's bringing a girl.

NIAMH   Nial?

TERESA   Yes.

NIAMH   He's bringing a girl here?

TERESA   Yes.

NIAMH   Wow! Who is she?

TERESA   She's… she's a girl he met in Cork.

NIAMH   A painter?

TERESA   I don't know, he didn't say.

NIAMH   Okay.

TERESA   But it's good news, isn't it, love?

NIAMH   Yeah. Yeah, I suppose it is.

TERESA	And I think there's to be a new exhibition of his work.
NIAMH	Yeah?
TERESA	In Spain.
NIAMH	Really.
TERESA	I think so, well, I'm not sure... but we can ask him all about it. Can't we... later?
NIAMH	Yeah.
	Though I don't know that I'll be here, I had planned to see a film after work.
TERESA	Oh, had you, love?... And are you meeting someone?
NIAMH	No.
TERESA	(*Registering disappointment*.) Oh.
	NIAMH *sighs*.
NIAMH	So what time is he coming?
TERESA	Teatime.
NIAMH	Ahhh...
	And is Ciara coming?
TERESA	Oh yes. Ciara.
NIAMH	So Ciara knows Nial is coming...
TERESA	She's making meringue.
NIAMH	Is she now.
	Pause.
TERESA	I think I'll have some shortcake.
	It will help me with the tablets.
NIAMH	Are you only taking your tablets now?

TERESA	Yes, I think I forgot them this morning.
NIAMH	Mam!
TERESA	Well, I was flustered with the trip to Tesco.
NIAMH	But you should have called – I would have gone for you or Ciara *should* have gone for you, where's your sheet?
TERESA	It's here. Don't fuss, Niamh, please.
NIAMH	But there's nothing marked for yesterday.
TERESA	Well, I took them yesterday, I know I did, I must just have forgotten to mark it.
NIAMH	Mam, you know how dangerous that is.
TERESA	Dangerous!
NIAMH	With your history.
TERESA	Stop it, Niamh.
NIAMH	You have to keep track of your tablets.
TERESA	And I do.
NIAMH	The doctor…
TERESA	I don't miss them ordinarily…
NIAMH	He said.
TERESA	I line them out… the blue then the pink and then the blue… and then I mark the sheet, ordinarily.
NIAMH	I know.
TERESA	It's regimental.
NIAMH	Well, it has to be, Mam.
	There is a 'beep beep' from the cooker and they both jump.
TERESA	That's the oven.
NIAMH	What?

TERESA   It's time to put in the quiche.

NIAMH   Okay, I'll do it?

TERESA   I feel exhausted.

           I think I should go for a rest, Niamh.

NIAMH   Charming –

TERESA   And sure you've got to get back to work.

NIAMH   I know.

TERESA   So I'll just lie down on the couch.

           And you might bring in my tea.

NIAMH   All right.

TERESA   And put the telly on for me, will you, Niamh...

           As they exit through the door.

           I can't manage it at all since Dave put in that
           box.

NIAMH   The Sky?

TERESA   Whatever it is, I can't seem to get any of the
           channels now.

           They are gone.

           The back door opens and CIARA *comes in with
           shopping bags.*

           She is unloading the shopping when NIAMH
           returns. CIARA *sees her and drops a carton of
           eggs.*

CIARA   Shit. Niamh!

NIAMH   What?

CIARA   You gave me a fright.

NIAMH   Sorry, I was in with Mam.

TERESA   (*Off.*) Who's that, love?

CIARA   It's only me, Mam.

TERESA   (*Off.*) Ciara?

NIAMH   Yes, it's Ciara, Mam.

TERESA   (*Off.*) Niamh's here.

CIARA   (*To* TERESA.) Yes!

               (*To* NIAMH.) Here, give me a hand so.

               They both clean up the mess.

               So how come you're here?

NIAMH   Just checking in.

CIARA   (*Surprised.*) Checking in?

NIAMH   And just as well. She had forgotten to take her tablets.

CIARA   Had she?

NIAMH   Yes.

CIARA   I don't think so.

NIAMH   You need to make sure she marks the sheet, Ciara!

CIARA   Oh, I do, do I?

NIAMH   Yes. We don't need her going gaga again.

CIARA   She's grand, Niamh.

NIAMH   Well, I was ringing all morning and she didn't answer!

CIARA   That's because she was in Tesco.

NIAMH   I know that now.

CIARA   I just hope she got eggs!

               She goes out to TERESA.

               NIAMH *roots through the bags.*

               CIARA *comes back in.*

*NIAMH sits down. There's a silence. CIARA
works preparing food throughout the following.*

Mam says you have to stay over?

NIAMH   Yeah.

CIARA   That's nice.

NIAMH laughs.

What?

NIAMH   Nial is coming. (*With sarcasm.*) Or didn't you
know?!

CIARA says nothing.

So why is he coming?

CIARA   (*Shrugs.*) I don't know.

I think he comes.

NIAMH   Here?

CIARA   Yes, of course here.

NIAMH   Really?

CIARA   Yes.

NIAMH   Regularly?

CIARA   No – the odd time.

NIAMH   And how do you know?

CIARA   Because she gets me to buy cake.

NIAMH   Christ!

And when did this start?

CIARA   Since the move to Cork I think, I don't know,
Niamh.

NIAMH   Well, why don't you ask her?

CIARA   Why don't you?

NIAMH	Because she talks to you.
	She doesn't talk to me…
CIARA	You don't give her a chance!…
NIAMH	She had her chance.
CIARA	Oh, come on, Niamh!

Silence.

NIAMH	So do you see him when he's here?
CIARA	No, I don't.
	I just know because of the cake.

Slight pause.

I haven't seen him since our wedding, Niamh, no more than you.

NIAMH	Right.

Slight pause.

She said he's bringing a girl.

CIARA	Yes.
NIAMH	That's it?
CIARA	What?
NIAMH	Well, what do you know about her?
CIARA	Nothing! Jesus, Niamh.
NIAMH	What?
CIARA	Would you listen to yourself… 'Who is she? What's he doing here?' He's her son.

Pause.

It's normal to come if you're a son, isn't it?

Pause.

I think it's good he's coming.

NIAMH   Do you?

CIARA   Yes and so does Dave.

NIAMH   Ahhhhhh.

CIARA   'Ahhhhh' what?

NIAMH   Dave thinks it's good he's coming.

CIARA   I'm not going to react to that.

          Pause.

          Are you going to be here for tea?

NIAMH   I have to stay over, don't I?

          But no, I won't be here for tea, no, I've something
          on.

CIARA   Oh...

NIAMH   Will you be here?

CIARA   I'm supposed to be working!

          She only landed this on me yesterday...

          NIAMH *doesn't acknowledge this as she knows*
          CIARA *will be there.*

NIAMH   And Dave?

CIARA   Yes.

NIAMH   Lovely.

CIARA   Look, it's one night. One tea, Niamh. Then he'll
          be gone.

NIAMH   Yes, like always.

          Pause.

          Are the kids coming over?

CIARA   No, they're with Dave's mam.

NIAMH   Oh... handy that...

> DAVE, CIARA*'s husband, enters through the back door.*

> Well, speak of the devil.

DAVE   Howaya, love.

          Hey, Niamh!

NIAMH   Hi, Dave.

TERESA   (*Off.*) Is that Niamh gone?!

CIARA   No, it's just Dave here, Mam.

DAVE   Didn't know you'd be here, Niamh.

NIAMH   I was just checking in.

DAVE   Right.

> *A look passes between him and* CIARA – NIAMH *never checks in.*

CIARA   Did you bring over that cutlery?

DAVE   I did.

CIARA   Good man.

DAVE   So, Niamh Lynch, how are ya?

NIAMH   I'm good.

DAVE   Lookin' great.

NIAMH   Thanks.

CIARA   Have you time for a sandwich, Dave?

DAVE /   Yeah!
NIAMH

> *They laugh under* CIARA*'s line.*

CIARA   You've got to be joking.

DAVE   Ahh sure, make her a sandwich, Ciara, we never see her.

CIARA   Exactly.

NIAMH   I'll just have whatever's going!

CIARA   There's nothing going.

DAVE   Ahh, go on, Ciara.

          CIARA *sighs*.

          So what's the news with you?

NIAMH   No news.

DAVE   I don't believe that.

NIAMH   I'm just busy with work.

DAVE   Yeah?

          CIARA *butts in on the conversation as she makes the sandwiches*.

CIARA   Was your mam all right with the kids, Dave?

DAVE   (*To* CIARA.) Delighted with them.

NIAMH   I've a launch on Monday.

DAVE   A launch?

CIARA   Even with the short notice?

DAVE   (*To* CIARA.) She didn't mind, she'd only her bridge to cancel.

CIARA   Oh no. Did you tell her it was last-minute, that we'd make it up to her?

DAVE   (*To* CIARA.) I did, she was grand about it.

          (*To* NIAMH.) A launch?

NIAMH   Yeah, it's a new book about Derry.

CIARA   Is that the one that you were editing, Niamh?

NIAMH   Yeah.

CIARA   Oh, well done, that's great that it got published.

NIAMH   Thanks.

DAVE	(*To* NIAMH.) And are they glamorous, these launches?
NIAMH	No.
DAVE	Free booze?
CIARA	Did you find Eoin's inhaler?
DAVE	(*To* CIARA.) I did.
NIAMH	No.
DAVE	(*To* NIAMH.) I can always be the man on your arm.
CIARA	Pyjamas?
DAVE	(*To* CIARA.) It was all in the bag.
NIAMH	Forget it, Dave.
CIARA	You're a gem.
DAVE	(*To* NIAMH.) Ahh, go on, I could do with a good night out.
NIAMH	I don't believe you need me for that.
DAVE	Ahh, ya see, it's all different now, Niamh, the kids, the mortgage… she has me under the whip!
NIAMH	You wish!
	They laugh.
CIARA	Ham, it'll have to do.
DAVE / NIAMH	Thanks.
NIAMH	So what about you?
DAVE	Ahhh, not a bother.
NIAMH	Still skiving!
DAVE	Of course.
NIAMH	Seen any good gigs?
DAVE	Gigs! Sure, how would I get out to gigs.

NIAMH	I'm sure you manage it.
DAVE	Who's been playin' in Whelan's?
NIAMH	I don't know, I'm telling you, it's all work.
CIARA	Would you don't be listenin' to her, Dave, she's out the whole time!
	Where are you off to tonight?
NIAMH	Just the pictures.
CIARA	See!
DAVE	On your own, is it?
NIAMH	Oh, would you stop fishing?
DAVE	Are we that obvious?
NIAMH	You, Dave, are always obvious.
	He laughs.
	TERESA *comes in.*
TERESA	Dave!
DAVE	Howaya, Teresa.
TERESA	Dave's here, Ciara.
CIARA	Yes.
TERESA	My goodness, it looks like we might have all the family this evening.
DAVE	Will we?
TERESA	Yes, Niamh is to stay over.
DAVE	Really?
TERESA	It's just a shame about the children.
DAVE	Ahh…
CIARA	But Dave's mother had them promised for today, Mam. She's been looking forward to it all week.

DAVE	So we couldn't disappoint her.
TERESA	Of course not.
	It just might have been nice for Nial to meet them.
NIAMH	(*Smiling.*) *Yes*.
CIARA	Well, maybe next time, Mam.
TERESA	Yes.
DAVE	So are ya having a cup of tea with us then, Teresa?
TERESA	No thanks, Dave, I'm having a lie-down.
	I just wondered if you'd gone back to work, Niamh.
NIAMH	I'm going in now after this sandwich.
TERESA	Oh, you got a sandwich?
CIARA	I made it.
TERESA	Ahh, you're a good girl, Ciara.
	Isn't she, Dave?
DAVE	The best.
TERESA	And you'll stay to do the arranging, won't you, love.
CIARA	Yes, Mam, so long as I get my shift covered...
TERESA	And will you be back for the tea, Dave?
DAVE	I will, T, sure I'm looking forward to seeing Nial.
TERESA	Oh, isn't that lovely.
NIAMH	You should go on back to the couch, Mam. Ciara has it all under control.
TERESA	It's a pity you can't join us, love.
NIAMH	Well, I'd no notice, had I, Mam?
	NIAMH *just watches the ball hop throughout all this.*

TERESA   Oh… you see –

CIARA   Don't mind her –

TERESA   Hah? –

CIARA   She'd the pictures planned, hadn't you, Niamh –
you'd never have made it.

TERESA   It's only a stopover.

DAVE   Of course it is. Niamh's only winding you up,
aren't ya, Niamh.

    You go and have your lie-down, T, and everything
will be grand.

CIARA   You need your rest, Mam.

TERESA   Oh, right so. (*To* NIAMH.) Dave might drop you
back, love.

CIARA   Sure he will.

DAVE   He will?

NIAMH   (*With a smile*.) Great, thanks!

DAVE   Jaysus.

    We better get going so.

CIARA   Thanks, I'll see you later.

TERESA   Do you have your key?

NIAMH   I do.

DAVE   See ya, girls.

CIARA   See ya, Dave. Come on, Mam, I'll bring you
inside.

    NIAMH *and* DAVE *are gone*.

TERESA   You'll make up the back room for Niamh, won't
you, Ciara.

CIARA   Yeah sure, Mam.

TERESA   Can you believe her arriving this morning?

          I mean, of all the mornings!

CIARA   I know.

TERESA   I wonder was it your father?

CIARA   What?

TERESA   All he ever wanted was the family together
          again.

CIARA   What?

TERESA   Is this some sort of sign?

CIARA   Oh, Mam!…

TERESA   That fortune is turning?

CIARA   I don't know…

TERESA   Well, first your brother rings!

          And then there's the news!

CIARA   What news?

TERESA   Well, the girl! He's never brought a girl, has he?

CIARA   No, but…

TERESA   Then Niamh arrives!

CIARA   But she just needed somewhere to stay.

TERESA   Maybe he thinks I should have asked her?

CIARA   Who?

TERESA   Your father.

CIARA   Ahhh, Mam.

TERESA   You see, he just loved us all together.

CIARA   (*Not so sure*.) Daddy did?

TERESA   Yes. (*Determinedly*.) Around the table.

CIARA   I don't remember that –

TERESA   And we never had that, not once after… after Nial, not even at the hospital.

CIARA   (*Non-committal.*) Right.

TERESA   I think he wants us all together… it's time now…

CIARA   Look, you just have your lie-down, Mam, and we'll see what happens.

TERESA   You might ring her for me, will you, Ciara… on the mobile…

CIARA   No, Mam, it's best to leave it.

TERESA   But you can always smooth things over, Ciara. Tell her I'd like us all together, I should have asked her –

CIARA   She's going out –

TERESA   Ask her nice.

CIARA   I'll see, okay…

TERESA   Good girl.

          As they go.

          And I've a rinse for my hair.

CIARA   Have you.

TERESA   Golden years, it was on special.

CIARA   Lovely.

TERESA   Lord God but you're the best, Ciara, you know that, don't you, love.

CIARA   Thanks, Mam.

TERESA   And I know your daddy's very proud.

          They are gone.

          There is a lighting change to denote a slight shift in time.

          Lights come back up.

> NIAL *and* RUTH *enter from the door, downstage left. They have come through the front door. They have some bags.*

NIAL   Mam!

RUTH   She's not here?

NIAL   Doesn't look like it.

RUTH   Oh.

NIAL   So you can relax.

RUTH   I am relaxed.

NIAL   Really?

RUTH   I am.

NIAL   You don't look relaxed.

RUTH   Stop!

> NIAL *laughs.*

> A little like you yesterday.

NIAL   What yesterday?

RUTH   Quaking.

NIAL   Well, of course I was…

RUTH   And now?

NIAL   Let's see…

RUTH   (*Moving in to him.*) Happy?

NIAL   Very happy.

> *They start kissing.*

RUTH   Oh, Nial. I can't quite believe it all, you know.

NIAL   Yeah.

RUTH   Wasn't it great to use the gallery for dinner?

> It felt just so, I don't know – white and right and spare and beautiful.

NIAL	(*With a small laugh.*) Did it.
RUTH	I just love going over the whole day in my mind.
	And you... standing there. Mine.
NIAL	Yours?
RUTH	Well, you just looked... beautiful too.
NIAL	Beautiful?
RUTH	Yes, beautiful.
	She is stroking his chest.
	With all the gang.
NIAL	I still don't know how you swung that one.
RUTH	I was right, though, wasn't I?
	It would have been lonely on our own.
NIAL	Not for me.
RUTH	But you enjoyed it.
NIAL	You know I did.
RUTH	See!
	I love your chest.
NIAL	Do you...
RUTH	You've such a great man-chest.
	She starts to kiss it. Then jumps.
	Who's that?
NIAL	(*Laughs.*) Who's what?
RUTH	Is it your mother?
NIAL	Where – under the table?
RUTH	I heard something.
NIAL	No, you didn't. Now go right back to where you were.

RUTH	But you better check!
NIAL	Then you'll go right back?
RUTH	Yes.

NIAL goes to the door but lifts up the tablecloth on his way, giving RUTH *a look that makes her laugh. He then calls through the door, downstage left.*

NIAL   Mam!

No answer. He shrugs his shoulders.

RUTH	Weird... I was sure I heard someone.
NIAL	She'll be back.
RUTH	Right.
NIAL	Now, where were we...
RUTH	Maybe we should make tea or something?
NIAL	What?
RUTH	Well, I'm afraid she'll come in now.
NIAL	Marvellous. Now you want some tea?
RUTH	Well, no, not really.
NIAL	Jesus, can you please tell me what it is we're doing here?
RUTH	You promised.
NIAL	I know I promised but... it's nuts.
RUTH	We're going on honeymoon...
NIAL	Exactly, so what do we want with this?
RUTH	I want to meet her, Nial.
NIAL	(*Moving in to her again.*) Okay. So meet her and we'll go. We'll get a little hotel in town like I said...

RUTH   Nooo – you always stay when you're in Dublin and that's important. I don't want her to think that's changing.

NIAL   But she didn't even know we'd be here.

RUTH   But she does now so it's too late.

NIAL   Really.

He starts to kiss her.

RUTH   For you to change your mind.

Another kiss.

Then he pulls back.

NIAL   Fuck this, come on.

RUTH   What?

NIAL   We're going to that hotel.

RUTH   No.

NIAL   She's not here.

RUTH   She's expecting us.

NIAL   We'll just slip into a taxi and...

RUTH   Shag.

NIAL   Pretty much.

RUTH   We can do that anyway, can't we?

NIAL   In me ma's house?

RUTH   Why not?

NIAL   Jesus, you've a lot to learn.

She moves away.

RUTH   I want to meet her, Nial, and your sister if she comes.

NIAL *sighs.*

NIAL   I know you do.

RUTH   I think it's important.

NIAL   I don't.

RUTH   But they're family now.

            NIAL *sighs*.

NIAL   Family.

            All right.

            Fuck it.

            NIAL *sits.* RUTH *stands. They are quiet but he is
            obviously not at ease in the space.*

RUTH   So what'll we do?

NIAL   Wait, I suppose.

RUTH   Wait?

NIAL   Well, I told you what I want to do.

            She ignores this.

RUTH   You did tell her what time?

NIAL   You heard me! You stood by the bloody phone!

            Pause.

RUTH   Will we put our stuff away?

NIAL   No.

RUTH   Why not?

NIAL   Because I don't know where she'll put us.

RUTH   Your room!

NIAL   I don't have a room. I never lived here.

RUTH   But when you stay?

NIAL   I'm in the spare room. I don't know. We'll wait till
            she gets back.

Pause. RUTH *starts to look around. She focuses
on framed pictures on the windowsill.*

RUTH   Who are they?

NIAL   Ciara's kids.

RUTH   Where are you?

NIAL   Don't know.

RUTH   Is that your dad?

          NIAL *stands up to take a look.*

NIAL   Yeah.

RUTH   You look like him.

NIAL   No, I don't.

RUTH   You do.

          NIAL *puts his arms around* RUTH. *He runs his
          hands down her side. She puts her arms back
          around his head. He kisses her neck. She arches
          back with her body.*

          When did you say he died?

NIAL   '99... heart attack.

RUTH   Oh yes. But he looks so fit there. Friendly.

NIAL   Right.

RUTH   And did they let you out for the funeral.

NIAL   (*Interrupted by this.*) ... Yeah.

RUTH   You never talk about him.

NIAL   No.

          I saw nothing of him. He worked.

RUTH   Where? Where did he work?

NIAL   In the bank. The bank was his world.

          Now, fuck this, I'd like us to go...

RUTH   No. No, I'm sorry, Nial. I'll stop.

NIAL   Too many questions…

RUTH   I know. I know. It's just being here, seeing their pictures. I can't help it. I've thought about it…

NIAL   You're no part of it, Ruth.

RUTH   I know that. But I want them to know, Nial, I want them to know how much I love you –

NIAL   There's no need –

RUTH   I want everyone to know –

NIAL   And I don't give a fuck about everyone. I only care about you.

RUTH   Trust me, Nial, this is important, it will give us the fresh start.

         NIAL *sighs*.

NIAL   I thought we had that.

RUTH   It will give us family.

         He sits.

         She starts to feel along the worktop.

         So where was the old house?

         Was it near?

NIAL   No, it wasn't near, it was the other side of the city.

RUTH   And have you ever been back?

NIAL   Now why the fuck would I go back?

RUTH   Sorry.

NIAL   Jesus.

RUTH   Nial!

NIAL   I don't think I can handle this.

RUTH	Shhh, please, I'm sorry.
NIAL	And I don't know how Ma's going to handle it.
RUTH	What?
NIAL	Us.
RUTH	Us?
NIAL	Yeah.
RUTH	But you said she was delighted with the news.
NIAL	Well!
RUTH	Well, what?
NIAL	She said she was.
RUTH	So?
NIAL	She's vulnerable, Ruth. Unpredictable.
RUTH	Really?
NIAL	I've told you that.
	She can hit the bed for days when... with anything new.
	So I don't know why the fuck we're here.
	Silent now.
	RUTH *shifts around a bit.*
	I just want me and you.
RUTH	It's just a visit –
NIAL	It's stirrin' is what it is, Ruth –
RUTH	It's normal to visit –
NIAL	I can feel it already – in the air, it'll just stir the shit up, I know it will.
RUTH	It was a long time ago, Nial, we both know that you're a different person now...

NIAL   (*Abruptly*.) Tsch, not here… never ever here!

RUTH   But I don't want us to hide…

NIAL   I don't fucking hide.

RUTH   I'm sorry.

NIAL   Now that's it.

            I want us to go.

            RUTH *doesn't move*.

            (*Eases*.) We can come again, okay.

            It's been a crazy week… and I don't feel ready for this.

            How about we come on our way back…

            There are sounds of someone outside.

            Oh, fuck it.

RUTH   Is it her?

NIAL   I'd say so.

RUTH   We'll be fine, Nial.

            No reply.

            I love you.

            The back door opens.

TERESA   Oh, Lord help us. You're here!

            You've not been waiting, have you?

NIAL   Howaya, Mam.

TERESA   They've been waiting here, Ciara!

CIARA   Hi, Nial.

NIAL   Ciara.

            She gives him a hug, which he is very awkward about.

TERESA   I had to go to the chemist, I'm so sorry.

NIAL   It's all right.

CIARA   She had a problem with her prescription…

TERESA   What must you think of us!

RUTH   We've only just arrived.

CIARA   Ahh, did you.

NIAL   Yeah.

TERESA   You see, I'd to switch my tablets, didn't I, Ciara.

CIARA   So I drove her.

TERESA   The new ones react with the bowel.

NIAL   Look, it's grand, Mam, we're grand.

              This is…

TERESA   The train must have been early, was it, son?

NIAL   No.

TERESA   God, I confused the times then, Ciara.

NIAL   Please don't be worrying, Mam, you're here now.

TERESA   Yes, yes I am. We all are.

NIAL   Yeah, and this is Ruth.

TERESA   Ruth.

RUTH   Yes.

TERESA   Well, it's just lovely to meet you, Ruth, to have
              you, isn't it, Ciara!

CIARA   Yes, absolutely. It is. It really is. And I'm Ciara,
              Nial's sister.

              They shake hands.

TERESA   Yes, and I'll put the kettle on, we'll put the kettle
              on, Ciara.

CIARA   Of course, sure you lot sit down, I'll do it...

TERESA   No no, we'll go into the living room.

NIAL   Here is fine.

RUTH   It's fine.

TERESA   Is it! But we haven't even cleared the table!

           CIARA *starts to clear and make tea. The other three sit or stand at the table.*

           Was your train early?

NIAL   No.

CIARA   Sit down, you guys. Are you hungry?

NIAL   No –

RUTH   No –

NIAL   We're grand –

RUTH   Thanks.

TERESA   But you must be parched after that long journey.

RUTH   Oh...

TERESA   They're parched, Ciara.

CIARA   Yes, well, I have the kettle on now.

NIAL   It's grand.

RUTH   I love the train.

TERESA   Do you?

RUTH   Yes.

CIARA   So do I, it's the only way to travel.

TERESA   Now!

           Pause.

RUTH   Yes.

           Pause.

CIARA   Well, it's great to see you, Nial.

NIAL   Yeah, great, Ciara.

CIARA   And to meet Ruth.

TERESA   Yes, Ruth.

               RUTH *smiles*.

NIAL   So how are you doing then?

CIARA   Good, great. Still in James'.

TERESA   Ciara's a nurse… cancer.

RUTH   Oh… lovely.

CIARA   And I still tolerate Dave!

NIAL   Ahh, great. (*To* RUTH.) Dave's a great guy.

TERESA   He's a tiler.

RUTH   Oh.

CIARA   He's coming over later, actually.

NIAL   Is he?

CIARA   Yeah –

TERESA   For the tea –

NIAL   Oh –

CIARA   He's looking forward to seeing you –

TERESA   I made quiche.

RUTH   Lovely.

TERESA   Yes.

RUTH   And it's so wonderful to finally meet you…
               Nial's told me so much about you all…

               Silence.

               Are they your two children in the picture,
               Ciara?

CIARA	Yeah –
TERESA	Yes, they're our babies, Eoin and Lill.
RUTH	Ahhhh.
TERESA	Bring over the picture, Ciara.
	CIARA *takes them off the windowsill for* RUTH.
RUTH	Oooooh, look. They look lovely, don't they, Nial.
NIAL	Yeah.
CIARA	They're divils –
TERESA	Angels!
RUTH	And am I going to meet them, then, this evening?
CIARA	Oh… no –
TERESA	No, they're at their gran's in Howth.
RUTH	Awwww.
CIARA	I'm sorry about that, you see, we didn't realise you'd be coming –
TERESA	And they were promised, weren't they, Ciara?
CIARA	Yes, they were, they were promised to Dave's mam. She dotes on them –
TERESA	Dotes –
RUTH	I'll bet. They look so lovely.
NIAL	And how are ya finding it then, Ciara, with the kids and all?
CIARA	Ah. It's grand. It's a bit of a juggle but we manage, Dave's mam is great, she minds them a lot.
RUTH	And you too I'll bet, Mrs Lynch.
TERESA	Oh… I just adore them –
CIARA	She adores them.

RUTH   Of course.

            Pause.

            So how old are they?

CIARA   Lill is three and Eoin's ten months.

RUTH   Wow! That's busy.

TERESA   It is –

CIARA   Ahh, it's grand.

TERESA   But she's a great mother.

            As well as a great daughter, I'll tell you, I'd be
            lost without her, Ruth, she does everything for me.

CIARA   Ahh, Mam.

RUTH   Ahhh.

NIAL   The little girl looks like ya, Ciara.

CIARA   Do you think so?

NIAL   Yeah, when you were small.

CIARA   Oh…

TERESA   Sure, she's the spit of you.

CIARA   You've never said that.

TERESA   Haven't I?

CIARA   No…

RUTH   We'd love to have kids, wouldn't we, Nial?

            Slight pause.

NIAL   Yeah.

CIARA   Really?

TERESA   Isn't that lovely.

CIARA   (*Quite surprised.*) Oh, lovely. Yeah.

NIAL   So are you still playing ball then, Ciara?

CIARA	God no… not since I had the kids.
NIAL	Ciara was a brilliant basketball player.
RUTH	Were you?
CIARA	Not brilliant.
NIAL	You played for Ireland!
CIARA	No, I didn't.
NIAL	I thought you did.
CIARA	Trials, I got trials.
TERESA	That's right. Trials.
CIARA	… Anyway, that was years ago. I stopped not long after really, haven't played for years.
NIAL	Oh right.
TERESA	Well, it's hard to keep it all going, love –
RUTH	Yes.
TERESA	The children take over.
CIARA	Well, I suppose. Between them and work –
NIAL	Yeah.
RUTH	Yes.
CIARA	But what about you, Nial? Mam tells us the painting's going really well.
NIAL	Ahh, yeah, I suppose it's all right.
RUTH	Better than all right!
CIARA	Yeah?
TERESA	Niamh read a review.
NIAL	Did she?
TERESA	In the *Irish Times*. We cut it out, didn't we, Ciara! It's in the top drawer.

RUTH	Oh, was it a recent one then?
TERESA	It's in the drawer –
CIARA	I don't know, a few weeks ago, I think, very impressive.
TERESA	Sure, get it out for Nial there, Ciara.
NIAL	No, it's all right, Mam, I'll have seen it.
TERESA	But it was a very good one: 'the extraordinary talent of Nial Lynch'…
CIARA	…'of Nial Lynch.'
TERESA	We were very proud, weren't we, Ciara.
RUTH	Oh, that was probably the Cells exhibition then – that's the one they're hanging in Spain.
TERESA	Cells?
RUTH	It's such a wonderful work.
TERESA	Is it?
RUTH	The great absence of light – and all the images merging to create this sense of incarceration, you know, of body and mind and soul, it's really… (*As she becomes aware of their nervous reaction.*) stunningly grim.
TERESA	Lovely.
CIARA	Yes.
NIAL	It's abstract, Mam.
RUTH	Very abstract.
CIARA	Well, it sounds fabulous.
TERESA	Doesn't it.
NIAL	Ahhh, it's all right.
	Slight pause.

TERESA	But isn't it great to find that talent –
RUTH	Oh yes, your son is becoming a major influence!
TERESA	Is he!
	Well!
	And you didn't draw at all when you were small!
	NIAL *does a short laugh.*
RUTH	Didn't he?
TERESA	No, it was Ciara was the drawer, wasn't it, love.
RUTH	Were you?
CIARA	I don't know.
TERESA	Yes, you won a prize in school for drawing – a plate thing!
CIARA	Jesus, that's right, how did you remember that, you're gas, Mam.
TERESA	Because it's in with all the basketball trophies, that's how. Taking over the whole cabinet!
	They all laugh a bit as the tension diffuses slightly.
CIARA	So are you a painter too then, Ruth?
RUTH	No. No.
NIAL	Yes you are.
RUTH	I try but compared to Nial my art is child's play.
NIAL	Your work is great.
RUTH	No it's not. I curate at the gallery.
TERESA	(*Not having a clue what that means.*) Oh… isn't that nice.
CIARA	And where's that?
NIAL	Kinsale.

CIARA   Oh, Kinsale is gorgeous –

TERESA   Lovely town.

RUTH   We premiere most of Nial's work.

CIARA   So is that where you met then, at the gallery?

RUTH   Yes, actually, it is.

TERESA   Ahhh, lovely.

CIARA   Yeah.

TERESA   Will you have a hot drop, Ruth?

RUTH   No thanks.

NIAL   Do you know we might just put up our bags, Ma.

TERESA   Oh yes, of course, son, settle in.

CIARA   Freshen up.

NIAL   Yeah.

RUTH   That'd be great.

TERESA   We made the bed up in the front room, Nial, we thought you'd be most comfortable there.

NIAL   Great.

TERESA   And Ciara will show Ruth the bathroom, won't you, love?

CIARA   Sure.

NIAL   Nah, don't worry, Ciara, I'll do it.

CIARA   Are you sure?

RUTH   Of course, we'll be fine.

TERESA   Do you need help with your bags?

NIAL   No, we're grand.

RUTH   Fine, thanks, Mrs Lynch.

TERESA   Teresa! Please.

RUTH   Okay, Teresa.

              They head out the door.

TERESA   You'll find your way…?

              They are gone.

CIARA   It's a three-bed semi, Mam!

TERESA   Go on up after them, Ciara, and see that
              everything's okay.

CIARA   Everything's grand, Mam.

TERESA   Did you put in the fresh towels –

CIARA   Yes. Now give them a breather?

TERESA   Do you think?

CIARA   Yes I do.

              TERESA *sits.*

TERESA   She seems nice enough, doesn't she?

CIARA   She's fabulous!

TERESA   Fabulous?

              But is she English?

CIARA   Absolutely she's English.

TERESA   So how did he meet an English one down there?

CIARA   Ahhh, Mam, for God's sake, there's English…
              there's people everywhere. (*And she laughs.*)

TERESA   But he never had any girl in London!

CIARA   You don't know that.

TERESA   I do, Ciara. I'm his mother.

CIARA   (*With cynicism.*) Right.

TERESA   But I will say he looks well on it, doesn't he,
              love?

CIARA   He does.

             (*Gently*.) He looks great, Mam.

TERESA   God. Your father'd be delighted.

CIARA   I don't think I've ever seen him look so well.

TERESA   No.

CIARA   I think he's happy.

TERESA   Oh, do you, Ciara?

CIARA   Yeah.

TERESA   Imagine! Nial. Happy!

CIARA   (*Touching her mother's hand tenderly*.) Yeah.

             Pause.

             CIARA *and* TERESA *start to organise tea things.*
             TERESA *catches sight of herself in a small*
             mirror.

TERESA   Mother of God, look at the state of me! Do you
             think I'll get a chance to put on a bit of lipstick,
             Ciara?

CIARA   Of course you will.

TERESA   But I don't want to disturb them.

CIARA   Sure, use the downstairs loo.

TERESA   Good idea... but my make-up bag is upstairs and I
             had wanted to change my top. Would I be in on
             top of them if I went up, do you think?

CIARA   No.

TERESA   I don't really want to be up after them.

CIARA   Oh, I'll go...

TERESA   Good girl, and see that everything is all right for
             them.

CIARA   Okay…

           She's gone. TERESA *stands at the door watching
           her go up. She comes back into the kitchen and
           goes to her handbag. She roots through it and
           finds an envelope, and goes to put it on the dresser
           when* NIAMH *comes in through the back door.*

TERESA   Niamh!

NIAMH   Hiya, Mam.

           TERESA *hurriedly puts the envelope back into
           her bag.*

TERESA   You came for the tea…

NIAMH   No, Mam, I didn't. I'm just looking for my purse.

TERESA   Your purse?

NIAMH   I think I left it here at lunchtime.

TERESA   Oh, but Nial is here, love!

NIAMH   He's here already!

TERESA   Yes, I think there was some mix-up with the train.

CIARA   (*Off.*) What top is it, Mam?

TERESA   (*To* CIARA.) What's that, love?

NIAMH   Well, I just want to pick up my purse and I'll be
           gone.

TERESA   Oh, don't go now, Niamh. Nial will want to see
           you…

CIARA   (*Off.*) What top?

TERESA   God, she'll disturb everyone, hold on a minute,
           Niamh, and I'll just go up to her.

NIAMH   No, I'm not stayin', Mam…

           TERESA *is gone.* NIAMH *goes to the counter to
           look for her purse, and* FIN *enters.*

FIN	Is it here?
NIAMH	Get out, Fin.
FIN	What?
NIAMH	I'm sorry, I just... I can't see it but do you mind waiting outside.
FIN	I do actually.
NIAMH	Please.
FIN	Jesus. Why do you always have me skulking around?
NIAMH	Because... Look, they've just gone upstairs...
FIN	So?
NIAMH	I don't want them to meet you.
FIN	Charming.
NIAMH	You know what I mean.
FIN	No, I don't know what you mean.
NIAMH	Mam will get all excited.
FIN	Over me?!
NIAMH	(*Laughs.*) Look, she's excitable, all right!
FIN	And you don't want them to know that we're together in work!
NIAMH	Nooo.
FIN	Why not?
NIAMH	Because! It's... well, it's our business.
	Now will you just wait outside or we'll get drawn into this.
FIN	Into what?
NIAMH	They're having tea. My sister's here.

FIN	Your sister? And is she as gorgeous as you?
NIAMH	My brother's coming.
FIN	Your brother? You never said you had a brother.
NIAMH	Didn't I? Well, he's coming to tea.
FIN	Great.
NIAMH	No, it's not great.

CIARA *comes in*.

CIARA	I thought you weren't coming…

(*To* FIN.) Oh, hi!

FIN	Hi.
NIAMH	This is a friend of mine, Ciara. Fin.
CIARA	Hi, Fin.
FIN	Hiya.
NIAMH	Fin's from the office.
CIARA	Is he?
FIN	Well, I wasn't born there but I do seem to spend most of my time at the desk!

CIARA *laughs politely*.

NIAMH	I just…

We just came back for my purse.

We're going to the IFI.

CIARA	Really!
NIAMH	With some friends.

Did you see it here, Ciara? I think I must have left it at lunchtime.

CIARA	No.
FIN	I'll give you a hand…

NIAMH	No –
CIARA	Sure.

They all have a look around. FIN *is all smiles to* CIARA.

Do you know that Nial is here?

NIAMH	Yeah, Mam said.
CIARA	She'd love you to stay.
NIAMH	I know.
FIN	We can if you like, Niamh.
NIAMH	No.
CIARA	And Ruth's here.
NIAMH	Ruth?
CIARA	The girl.
NIAMH	Oh right, what's she like?
CIARA	She's fabulous.
FIN	Fabulous!

TERESA *come in, she has the new top on.*

TERESA	There, is that any better, girls?
	Oh?
FIN	Hello.
CIARA	This is –
FIN / NIAMH	Fin.
FIN	Pleased to meet you.
TERESA	Oh.
CIARA	A friend of Niamh's.
TERESA	Well!...

NIAMH	We just came back for my purse, like I said, but I can't seem to find it.
TERESA	Oh dear.
CIARA	You probably left it in Dave's car!
NIAMH	Oh, that's it, I bet I did.
TERESA	Well, ring him then, Ciara.

CIARA *exits with her mobile*.

Fionn can have a cup of tea.

FIN	Oh, that'd be lovely.
NIAMH	But we're supposed to be going to the pictures, Mam... we've to meet someone.
TERESA	There's always time for a cup of tea!

And your brother's here.

FIN	We can always text the others.
TERESA	There.

RUTH *and* NIAL *come in*.

Look! Niamh came to see you, son.

NIAL	Niamh!
TERESA	And this is Ruth.
RUTH	Hi.
NIAMH	Hi.

As CIARA *returns*.

RUTH	Wow, it's a full house.
TERESA	Yes, we like to get together.

This is a friend of Niamh's.

FIN	Fin.
RUTH	Hi, Fin, how are you?

He smiles to CIARA.

FIN   Fabulous!

She gives him a grin.

CIARA   Dave has your purse, Niamh. You left it in his
           car.

NIAMH   Did I? Shit.

FIN   Well, at least you know where it is.

TERESA   Exactly, love.

CIARA   And he'll be here any minute.

NIAMH   Okay.

CIARA   Was everything all right for you guys?

NIAL   Great, yeah –

RUTH   Perfect.

CIARA   Right, well…

TERESA   We're all here now.

CIARA   Yes, we are.

TERESA   Except Dave!

CIARA   Any minute!

RUTH   Wonderful.

CIARA   So I'll set the tea.

RUTH   I'll give you a hand.

TERESA   Oh no, no. Niamh will, won't you, love…

NIAMH   Em… okay, but remember, Mam, I've
           arrangements…

NIAL   Yeah, don't be worrying about us.

RUTH   No.

NIAMH   No.

TERESA   And sure, Fionn here said you can e-mail them!

FIN   Text.

TERESA   Exactly.

FIN   There's a gang going so they won't miss us.

NIAMH   No.

CIARA   You'll stay for a while.

NIAMH   Yeah, for a while... and then we'll go.

TERESA   Of course.

RUTH   Great.

FIN   Perfect.

TERESA   The whole family.

           Your father will be delighted.

           (*To* RUTH.) He just loved us all together.

RUTH   And I'm sorry he's not still with us, Mrs Lynch.

           TERESA *takes* RUTH*'s hand and squeezes it.*

CIARA   So!

           Would anyone like a drink?

FIN   Eh, yeah, that'd be great.

TERESA   What do we have, Ciara?

CIARA   Beer or wine!

NIAL   I'll have a beer, Ciara, here, where are they? Sure, I'll get one myself.

TERESA   No, no, you sit down, Nial. Niamh will get it, won't you, Niamh!

CIARA   (*To* NIAMH.) Beers in the fridge.

           (*To* TERESA.) Sit down yourself now, Mam, and relax.

           NIAMH *goes to the fridge.*

TERESA   I will.

My goodness, such a hive of activity.

There are some conversations overlapping now. Those in bold are the ones that the audience hear and the others play out in the background with the characters tuning in and out of each dialogue as they would in any real situation – often participating in two conversations at once.

RUTH   **Will I set the table?**

TERESA   **Oh no, you're a guest, Ruth.**

RUTH   **(*To* TERESA.) Oh, but I'm happy to help.**

(*To* CIARA.) What would you like me to take down for you?

CIARA   The salads would be great.

RUTH   Oh, lovely, such sweet tomatoes.

CIARA   Yes, there's a little organic market in the village.

RUTH   Is there, you lucky thing… There is a market in Kinsale but I never seem to get to it and I just love these little vine tomatoes.

She tastes one.

Oh, there is just no comparison, is there!

TERESA   **I don't think there's ever been so many of us.**

CIARA   **No.**

(*And she continues her tomato chat with* RUTH.) I just added a little salt and olive oil.

RUTH   Gorgeous.

FIN   **Could I have a glass of red, do you think?**

NIAMH *glares at him.*

TERESA   **Certainly… Niamh!**

NIAMH *goes to open a bottle on the counter.*

And I made quiche.

FIN	**Lovely.**
NIAL	**Great, Mam –**
TERESA	**So you and Niamh are friends, Fergus?**
FIN	**Yes.**
CIARA	(*As she drops something to the table.*) **Fin.**
FIN	**We work together.**
TERESA	**Oh, do you?**
NIAL	**Where's that?**
TERESA	**Niamh's in a small publishing house now, Nial. It's small but very successful.**
NIAL	**Really?**
RUTH	**Exciting.**
NIAMH	**Not really, I'm just in the office.**
TERESA	**And two degrees!**
FIN	**And we're in a writers' group together.**
RUTH	**Are you?**
FIN	**Yes.**
RUTH	(*To* FIN.) So what do you write?
FIN	Oh, lots, I try to write every day.
RUTH	Do you?
FIN	I'm working on a novel at the moment.
RUTH	How interesting…
FIN	It's kind of comic, two guys on a scam.
RUTH	Wow, how do you even start!
NIAL	(*To* NIAMH.) **So you're still writing then?**

NIAMH	No.
CIARA	You are, Niamh!
NIAMH	Not really.
RUTH	(*Piping in from her conversation with* FIN.) And what about you, Niamh, what do you write?
NIAMH	Nothing much.
FIN	(*To* RUTH.) Short stories are terrific…
NIAL	Are they?
RUTH	I'll bet.
NIAMH	They're largely unfinished.
FIN	She'll rarely let anyone read them.
RUTH	Why's that?
FIN	That's just Niamh, but she'll come round, she'll have to… they're amazing.
RUTH	Yes.
TERESA	And what was that course you went on in the summer, love?
NIAMH	What?
TERESA	The one in Mayo?
NIAMH	Oh, that was an arts centre – a residence.
TERESA	A 'singles' week', wasn't that it, love?
NIAMH	What?
TERESA	For people on their own?
NIAMH	Jesus, what gave you that idea?
TERESA	Your sister…
CIARA	I just said it was the kind of place you might meet someone.
NIAMH	Jesus, Ciara.

CIARA	With similar interests, I never said it was a singles' week.
NIAMH	It was a writing week.
TERESA	And is that where you met Fionn?
FIN	No!
NIAMH	Fin.
	DAVE *comes in through the back door.*
DAVE	Howayiz.
CIARA	Oh, Dave –
TERESA	Dave!
DAVE	Jaysus, what a gang!
CIARA	Hi, love.
NIAL	Hiya, Dave.
NIAMH	Dave.
DAVE	Ahhh, Nial. It's great to see you, man!
NIAL	Yeah, you too, Dave…
TERESA	Sit in here, Dave, next to Nial and Ruth.
DAVE	Oh, Ruth.
NIAL	Yeah, this is Ruth.
RUTH	Hiya.
DAVE	Well, hello there!
TERESA	And this is a friend of Niamh's, Dave.
NIAL / RUTH / CIARA	Fin!
DAVE	Right, Jaysus, it's a party.
TERESA	Isn't it!

CIARA	**We were just setting up.**
RUTH	Do you want to keep the deserts till after?
CIARA	Yeah, just leave them on the counter.
DAVE	**I can see that, fair play to yiz.**
TERESA	**There's quiche.**
DAVE	**And beer I see. I'll have one of them!**
TERESA	**Niamh, love, will you get Dave a beer?**
	NIAMH *gets up grudgingly to get a beer.*
CIARA	You might just throw a few more in the fridge as well, Niamh.
RUTH	Gosh, you've gone to a lot of trouble, Ciara.
CIARA	Ahh now, it was mostly Mam.
DAVE	**So, Nial! Look at you, you're gone all artist on us.**
FIN	**Artist?**
NIAL	**Am I?**
CIARA	**I think it's the shirt!**
RUTH	**I bought him that shirt!**
	They laugh and return to their background dialogue.
DAVE	**Jaysus.**
TERESA	(*To the girls.*) **And I think it's a lovely shirt.**
NIAL	**So it's been a while!**
DAVE	**It has, and how are things in Cork?**
NIAL	**Pretty good…**
DAVE	(*Nodding to* RUTH.) **I can see that!**
CIARA	**We saw that, Dave!**

TERESA	He's having an art exhibition in Spain, aren't you, Nial!
DAVE	Jaysus, yeah?
CIARA	That's where they're flying to tomorow.
DAVE	Very nice!
	How long are you going for?
RUTH	(*Putting her arms around* NIAL*'s neck.*) Three whole weeks!
CIARA	Ooooh, that's fantastic.
RUTH	Yes, I know.
FIN	So you're an artist, Nial?
RUTH	The exhibition is in Girona and then we hope to travel about a bit.
TERESA	Nial's a painter, Fionn... and very successful.
FIN	Wow! Really?
DAVE	Oh, I'll tell ya... this here's the next Louis le Brocquy, isn't he, T!
FIN	So what kind of art is it, Nial?
NIAL	Mostly abstract.
FIN	Fab!
	And do you work in oils or –
NIAL	Yeah, mostly.
RUTH	You can see Nial's work online... 'Cora Gallery'.
FIN	Fantastic, I'll have to look it up...
NIAMH	I've seen it.
NIAL	Have you, Niamh...?
NIAMH	Yes.

She gives no further comment.

FIN   Wow, Niamh, you never said!

CIARA   I didn't know it was online?

RUTH   Oh yes, there's always a selection of art from the gallery.

             But you'll have to come see it properly for yourself.

FIN   That'd be great!

             He looks to NIAMH, *delighted with himself. She just ignores him.*

TERESA   Yourself and Dave should go to Cork, Ciara.

CIARA   Ooooh, we'd love to, wouldn't we, Dave!

NIAMH   Mam would take the kids!

TERESA   Do you know I would, Niamh, I'm better able these days and you know I'd be delighted to have them.

DAVE   Of course you would, T.

             Jaysus, we might just think about that, hey, Ciara?

CIARA   A second honeymoon.

RUTH   Yes, and we'd never see you at the gallery!

             Laughter.

TERESA   Nial had a review in the *Irish Times*, Fin.

FIN   Did he?

TERESA   It's in the drawer!

             We have it cut out.

             Niamh will show it to you, won't you, Niamh.

             NIAMH *ignores this.*

FIN   Great.

NIAL   So what are you at, Dave?

DAVE   Ahh, still kicking about, few beers, few gigs...
             few kids!...

NIAL   I heard!

RUTH   We were looking at pictures.

DAVE   Oh yeah, their granny has them plastered all
             over the house.

TERESA   Get the pictures of Eoin's christening, will you,
             Ciara, they're in the dresser.

DAVE   Ahh now, we don't want to be boring the good
             people with albums, Teresa.

CIARA   Well, that's it, guys, that's the tea set.

             Thanks for all your help, Ruth.

TERESA   Yes, Ruth... and you a guest!

RUTH   No problem.

DAVE   Sit down, love.

NIAL   Yeah, sit down, Ciara.

CIARA   Right.

DAVE   Are you having a glass of wine, T?

TERESA   God, I might.

DAVE   Sure, why wouldn't ya?

TERESA   Well, you did a great job, girls.

NIAL   Yeah.

CIARA   Just help yourselves.

ALL   Lovely, thanks. (*Etc.*)

DAVE   Jaysus, remind me to give you your purse, Niamh,
             it's in me jacket.

NIAMH	Yes, thanks, Dave, coz we're not staying…
FIN	**So does your exhibition open tomorrow?**
NIAL	**Monday.**
RUTH	**We're just going over early to be sure that they've hung it properly, and Nial will have to do a few interviews.**
TERESA	**And do you mind that, son.**
NIAL	**No.**
RUTH	**They are not at all invasive, Teresa.**
TERESA	**Oh.**
FIN	It must be amazing. To have your work showing in Spain.
DAVE	Yeah, it's a great spot…
FIN	**And will it tour anywhere else?**
RUTH	**Possibly San Francisco.**
CIARA	**Wow –**
FIN	**Fantastic –**
TERESA	**Oh my goodness –**
RUTH	**You see, we have a relationship with this gallery in Girona and they regularly take Irish art –**
TERESA	**The very best, is it, love?**
RUTH	**Oh yes, and of a style. It's a co-curate, a mix of Irish and Catalan art –**
DAVE	**Jaysus, well done, Nial –**
RUTH	**And there is this Hispanic gallery in San Fran expressing an interest.**
DAVE	**Ah, forget Cork, we'll go see your pictures in the States, won't we, Ciara!**
CIARA	**Too right.**

More laughter.

So how did you get involved in all this, Ruth?

RUTH   From art college, really.

DAVE   And where was that, Ruth? **You're not from Cork!**

RUTH   **You guessed?**

Another small laugh.

I'm from Chichester –

TERESA   **Oh, isn't that nice –**

RUTH   **It's a small town south of London.**

FIN   I think my parents have been there.

TERESA   Have they, Fin?

FIN   Ahh yes, they go to England regularly.

DAVE   I don't know it, **have you been over, Nial?**

NIAL   **No.**

RUTH   **It's in the Downs.**

TERESA   **Oh, lovely.**

CIARA   **Gorgeous... and are you long living in Cork?**

RUTH   **About two years.**

CIARA   **Is that all?**

RUTH   **Well, my mum's from there so I've been over and back since I was a kid.**

TERESA   **Oh, your mother is, really?**

RUTH   **Yes, she's from Mallow.**

TERESA   **And does she like England.**

RUTH   **Oh yes, that's totally home now.**

CIARA   I hear it's a beautiful part of England.

RUTH	Yes, it's really pretty.
TERESA	**Imagine!**
	Did you get some potato salad, Nial.
NIAL	**I did, Ma, thanks.**
TERESA	**And quiche.**
RUTH	**It's all delicious.**
ALL	**Yes. (*Etc.*)**
TERESA	**Well, it's just a bit of a buffet.**
DAVE	**It's great it is, well done, T.**
NIAMH	**So you're away in the morning?**
NIAL	**Yeah, Niamh – the flight's at around ten.**
RUTH	**So we thought it might be nice to visit tonight –**
TERESA	**And I was delighted, wasn't I, Ciara –**
CIARA	**Yeah –**
DAVE	Fair play to ya.
TERESA	**So will you be working over there then, son?**
NIAL	**A bit of work, Ma, and a bit of a holiday.**
RUTH	**Definitely a holiday!**
FIN	**I believe it's a beautiful town, Girona.**
RUTH	Yes.
FIN	Picasso!
RUTH	Exactly.
FIN	He's associated with that area, isn't he?
NIAMH	Yes.
DAVE	**Anywhere in Spain's nice… We went to… where was it, Ciara?**
CIARA	**Torrevieja.**

DAVE	Yeah… great spot.
RUTH	That's just south, actually, a few hours from where we'll be staying.
DAVE	Is it, yeah?
	Well, it was well set up it was – pool, bars… the whole lot.
TERESA	Lovely.
	Have some more potato there, Fionn.
FIN	No thanks, Mrs Lynch, it was just delicious, I'm stuffed.
CIARA	Well, you'll have another glass of wine?
RUTH	It's lovely wine – oh, Spanish!
FIN	Great, I will, thanks!
	So are you guys in Dublin regularly then?
NIAL	No –
RUTH	Not really, no, though Nial has to come up sometimes to meet with agents and auctioneers.
CIARA	Do you, Nial?
NIAL	Yeah, just the odd time.
TERESA	So it's hard to get us all together!
	What about your family, Fionn?
FIN	Ahh yeah, the same, we're a bit scattered.
DAVE	Anyone want another beer?
NIAL	Yeah, I'll have one, thanks, Dave.
FIN	I've a sister in the States.
TERESA	Have you?
FIN	And another in Belfast but there's a brother at home in Sutton.

TERESA	Sutton! Are you from Sutton?
FIN	Yeah.
TERESA	Oh.
NIAMH	Ciara spent a lot of time out there –
CIARA	When I was young –
TERESA	With my sister, Rita –
FIN	Whereabouts –
DAVE	There you go, Nial... Corona, is that all right?
NIAL	Yeah, great, Dave.
CIARA	Sutton Cross.
FIN	Oh, we live just on the Howth Road.
TERESA	Really! (*To* NIAMH.) The Howth Road! Lovely.
NIAMH	You even went to school out there at one stage, didn't you, Ciara.
CIARA	Just for a few months.
DAVE	So this is quite an occasion, isn't it, T, having Nial over!
TERESA	Oh yes, I suppose...
DAVE	We should drink to it! And to it happening more often!
TERESA	Oh yes, let's... cheers.
ALL	Cheers, *Sláinte*. (*Etc.*)
DAVE	Ruth will see to it, won't you, Ruth?
RUTH	Oh yes... and well... actually, this is a bit of an occasion, isn't it, Nial!
CIARA	Oh!

There's a silence.

NIAL *doesn't reply.*

RUTH	Nial and I got married yesterday.
	Big pause and then overlapping reactions.
NIAMH	Married?
CIARA	Really –
NIAMH	Jesus –
TERESA	Yes –
FIN	Congratulations.
DAVE	Jaysus, yeah!
CIARA	So when, so… so when was the wedding?
NIAL	Yesterday.
CIARA	Oh, sorry, of course it was yesterday!
	Isn't that what you just said!
RUTH	Yeah.
	Small laugh.
CIARA	I can't believe it.
DAVE	Wow, that's great, Nial.
TERESA	I'm just delighted for you, son.
NIAMH	Yep.
CIARA	(*To* TERESA *in surprise.*) Did you know about this, Mam?
TERESA	Well, I wasn't sure if I heard Nial correctly on the phone but…
DAVE	You see, she's a dark horse, aren't you, Teresa.
CIARA	How on earth did you keep that to yourself?
TERESA	But you see, you know me, love, I could have got it all wrong.
DAVE	Now, Teresa!

TERESA	And then everyone would have been all excited and… anyway… it's nice to be able to say it for yourself, isn't it, Ruth!
RUTH	Oh, it is, thank you, Mrs Lynch.
CIARA	Oooh, this is so exciting, I feel I want to give you a big hug.
DAVE	Sure do, for God's sake.
	CIARA *and* RUTH *hug.*
	Lots of 'oohs'.
	Fair play, Nial.
NIAL	Well, it was just us. Just quiet. And then we're heading away tomorrow. You know, no fuss.
RUTH	No –
TERESA	Of course –
CIARA	Yes –
DAVE	Well, we'll have to celebrate tonight.
CIARA	Oh, we will, I can't believe it.
NIAMH	So did you have the wedding in Cork?
NIAL	Yeah, yeah, we did, Niamh –
TERESA	Lovely –
CIARA	And when did you get engaged?
RUTH	In June. We're together since –
NIAL	Christmas.
RUTH	Yes, Christmas Eeeeeve…
CIARA	Oh.
DAVE	Quick off the mark there, weren't ya, Nial.
NIAL	Yeah.

DAVE	And who could blame ya!
TERESA	**Myself and your father married in six months.**
NIAMH	We know.
RUTH	**Did you?!**
FIN	**So you're keeping up a family tradition, Nial.**
NIAL	**Yeah, I suppose.**
	FIN *looks to* **NIAMH.** *She nearly chokes on her wine.*
TERESA	Love at first sight. Kevin always said that.
RUTH	**So where did you meet, Teresa?**
TERESA	**The Four P's.**
	It was a dance on Harcourt Street.
DAVE	**Well, I'd say he's a happy man tonight, T, your Kevin.**
TERESA	**Yes, I'm sure he is, Dave.**
	I'm sure he's very proud.
CIARA	Mam.
	She takes TERESA*'s hand.*
	NIAMH *sighs in disgust.*
NIAL	**Yeah, well, we're just, you know, it was just quiet.**
RUTH	**A small ceremony and dinner with friends –**
NIAL	**In Kinsale.**
CIARA	**Oh, that sounds lovely –**
FIN	**Yeah –**
DAVE	**Fantastic –**
CIARA	**And so intimate!**

RUTH   It was, Ciara, and that was the really magic thing about it.

CIARA   Oh, I bet.

NIAMH   And did any of your family go?

RUTH   No.

NIAMH   Oh, how come?

DAVE   Ahh, they just kept it quiet, Niamh.

NIAL   Yeah.

RUTH   Just us.

DAVE   And weren't you dead right.

Sure, it gets crazy with the big weddings, doesn't it.

CIARA   Crazy –

TERESA   And very expensive –

CIARA   Yes –

NIAL   Yeah, all that.

NIAMH   But I'm sure Mam would have gone down.

Worn the hat!

NIAL   It wasn't that kind of day.

NIAMH   No?

CIARA   And what did you wear, Ruth?

RUTH   Oh, just a summer dress, I got it in Jigsaw in Cork, cerise pink! I'll have it for Spain.

TERESA   I'm sure you looked beautiful.

CIARA   Yes.

TERESA   Have you any photos?

RUTH   We do –

CIARA   Oh, we'll have to see them.

DAVE   Ahhh, there ya go, T.

RUTH   We'll send them on when we get them developed.

NIAMH   I'm sure Mam would have loved to have seen you.

TERESA   Not at all.

RUTH   Oh, I'm sorry, you know… that you weren't there, Teresa, but…

NIAL   We wanted to keep it…

DAVE   Quiet, yeah.

           Sure, we'd never of managed to get down anyway, would we, Ciara? With the kids and all.

CIARA   No, probably not.

TERESA   And work!

DAVE   (*To* CIARA.) It's hard to shift the shifts, isn't it, love.

TERESA   It is, Dave.

NIAMH   And did your own mother not go then?

RUTH   No.

NIAMH   Oh.

TERESA   Sure, **it would be too far for her to travel, Niamh.**

DAVE   Exactly, yeah.

NIAMH   Or your dad?

CIARA   Niamh!

RUTH   Mum's on her own, actually.

TERESA   Oh, is she, love?

RUTH	Yes. She raised me herself.
DAVE	A great woman, obviously –
RUTH	Yeah, she is –
CIARA	You must be very close –
RUTH	Yes, we are –
CIARA	Of course you are –
TERESA	Lovely –
NIAMH	Gosh! Yet she didn't go to your wedding!
CIARA	Jesus, Niamh –
FIN	Niamh!
RUTH	It's all right. Mum wouldn't come because…
NIAL	Ruth, you don't have…
RUTH	She thinks the marriage is a big mistake because of Nial's history.

Big pause from everyone.

But I know she'll come round because I know the man Nial is and I love him and I wanted you all to know that. And that's really why we're here.

Pause.

NIAL	(*Under his breath.*) Christ.

Big pause.

CIARA	Well, thanks, Ruth.
DAVE	Yes.
TERESA	Thank you, love.
CIARA	And we're really delighted he's found someone like you.
DAVE	Yeah. Here's to ya!

TERESA is getting upset.

NIAMH	**Jesus.**
CIARA	**Would anyone like meringue?**
NIAMH	**Oh, for fuck's sake, Ciara.**
TERESA	**Stop it, Niamh.**
NIAMH	**Well, Jesus Christ. Meringue! Nial's history! This is so fucking rich.**
RUTH	**I'm sorry, I didn't mean…**
NIAMH	**And what exactly is it you know then, Ruth?**
TERESA	Stop it.
RUTH	**Sorry?**
NIAMH	**About Nial's 'history'?**
NIAL	**Don't engage with her, Ruth.**
NIAMH	**Oh, that's right, Nial – don't engage – it's always worked for you.**
DAVE	Will you just sit down, Niamh –
NIAMH	**I want to know what is it you know?**
RUTH	**I know all of it –**
TERESA	**I'm afraid I don't feel very well –**
RUTH	**But Nial's a different man now.**
CIARA	It's all right, Mam.
NIAMH	**You know nothing –**
NIAL	We're going –
RUTH	**I know she was your friend, Niamh.**
	And I can understand that hurt.
NIAMH	**Hilary, her name was Hilary.**
CIARA	**Please stop this now!**

TERESA	Oooooh God.
CIARA	It's all right, Mammy.
DAVE	You're all right, T.
NIAMH	You understand nothing.
	And you know nothing.
	Because Nial knows fucking nothing.
NIAL	Right, come on.
TERESA	No!
NIAL	We're not listening to this, Mam.
NIAMH	No, of course you're not.
NIAL	I don't owe you anything, Niamh.
NIAMH	You owe me everything –
DAVE	Jesus, Niamh.
NIAMH	What do you think our lives were like when you went '*away*', Nial, what do you think?
CIARA	For God's sake, Niamh, not now.
NIAMH	Not now? When then? He fucking swans in here with his abstract art and his miracle girl and I'm supposed to be happy, is that it?
NIAL	I'm sorry, Ma…
TERESA	Nial, please –
NIAMH	Oh, that's it, Nial, just head back to Cork or Spain or wherever it is, this bright new life they've handed you, and leave us to live your shit.
NIAL	No one's fucking handed me anything.
RUTH	Nial's worked really hard…
NIAMH	Oh, spare me, please.

DAVE	Jesus, lads, calm down.
NIAMH	No, I'm tired of it, Dave. Tired of all the pretence.
DAVE	There's no pretence, for God's sake, Niamh, can we all just get on with it…
NIAL	I'm sorry, Mam, we're going.
TERESA	No, love, no.
CIARA	Hold on, Nial.
	It's all right, Mam.
RUTH	I'm sorry, Mrs Lynch, I really didn't mean…
TERESA	No, don't be sorry –
NIAMH	She's right, don't be sorry, Ruth, because for years we've had to swallow Nial's 'history'.
DAVE	Niamh!
NIAMH	But now you with your wide-eyed pretty fucking resilience have just spewed it up all over the tea!
TERESA	Ooooooh God.
	TERESA *throws up her quiche*.
DAVE	For fuck's sake.
CIARA	Mammy!
FIN	Jesus, she's been sick.
NIAMH	Perfect.
	FIN *is up with puke all down his trousers*. DAVE *switches between attending to* TERESA *and tackling* NIAMH. RUTH *is just astonished by what she has unleashed*.
	Not even Mammy can stomach it any more!
NIAL	You're a stupid bitch, Niamh.

CIARA   It's all right, Mammy.

TERESA   Oh God, Ciara... I feel faint, love.

CIARA   Dave, give me a hand, will you.

DAVE   There you go, T.

FIN   Niamh, your mother, Jesus –

NIAL   You always were –

CIARA   Get them to stop, Dave –

NIAMH   I can't believe he has the balls to come here –

DAVE   Stop this, now, Niamh.

     TERESA *heaves again.*

CIARA   Oh God, Mammy.

RUTH   You'll need to call a doctor.

TERESA   I just can't stop.

     She heaves again.

NIAMH   After everything.

RUTH   Please... Here, I'll get towels.

NIAMH   Don't bother. It's just a diversion.

FIN   Jesus.

RUTH   She's sick.

NIAMH   She isn't.

     She takes **TERESA** *quite violently by the chin.*

CIARA   Niamh!

**NIAMH   It's always the same, isn't it, Mam – resort to
     the pills or the puke because otherwise you'll
     have to look at it, won't you! Look at us and
     see... really see.**

CIARA   Stop it.

NIAMH	How he fucking destroyed us and how you never saved us...
	DAVE *intervenes, roughly pulling* NIAMH'*s hand away from* TERESA.
	TERESA *starts to sob*.
DAVE	Jesus Christ, Niamh.
NIAMH	He killed Hilary.
DAVE	Yeah, and we all know that.
NIAMH	Well, that's not just history.
RUTH	Please...
NIAMH	Is it, Nial?
TERESA	Ooooooh God.
CIARA	It'll be all right, Mam.
DAVE	Well, are you happy now?
	Do you feel better for that, Niamh?
	TERESA *heaves again*.
FIN	Don't you think you should call a doctor?
	Blackout.
	End of Act One.

ACT TWO

We are back in the kitchen as it was before the interval, but the lighting state is notably different. We are witnessing NIAMH*'s memory of herself and* HILARY *early on the day of the murder, but the audience do not see* NIAMH *at first. All they see is a twelve-year-old girl dancing to music – an obviously well-rehearsed routine.*

The young girl dances and talks to a young NIAMH *as if she was beside her. Older* NIAMH *slowly engages in the scene, watching* HILARY *all the time, and answering as young* NIAMH *but not physically taking up the position.*

HILARY   Why does Grainne have to go to piano today of all days, Niamh? She should be here to practise the routine.

NIAMH   I know.

HILARY   She should have just made her mam let her skip it.

NIAMH   Yeah.

HILARY   Now she'll be way behind.

We could lose because of her, you know.

She could wreck everything.

NIAMH   Maybe we should ditch her?

HILARY   Maybe we should.

Now twirl.

She twirls and bumps bums as if the young NIAMH *were dancing with her.*

NIAMH   And her legs look terrible in the skirt.

HILARY   They do. They're all bruises after the hockey.

> So that's it, she's gone.

NIAMH   Grand.

HILARY   Now put the track back to the start, and we can work our way through into the swing with no Grainne.

NIAMH   Okay.

HILARY   From the top.

> Forward – Back, two, three.

NIAMH   You do that flip much better than me, Hil.

HILARY   No I don't.

NIAMH   You do.

HILARY   You look great.

NIAMH   I'm just so afraid I'll forget the steps.

HILARY   Focus on the music, that's what Mrs Martin said.

NIAMH   But all those people.

HILARY   They'll love us!

> Come on, we'll do it again. Feet together – Cross – Turn.

> There, you got it that time.

NIAMH   I did, didn't I!

HILARY   Of course you did.

NIAMH   Grainne never got it.

HILARY   No. Now we'll go again from the start, put the track back.

NIAMH   Sure.

> HILARY *is getting into position*.

> You know you look amazing, don't you.

HILARY   Amazing!

NIAMH   Your hair is fab.

HILARY   Thanks.

NIAMH   What will I be like?!

           The outfit looks so much better on you.

HILARY   Niamh! I think you look fab too.

NIAMH   Do you?

HILARY   Of course I do. Now come on and we'll do the shake.

           She does this kind of bum-shake, singing the song and laughing. NIAMH *laughs watching her.*

           HILARY *hits the floor now, tired from the dancing.*

           What time is your mam back?

NIAMH   I dunno, she's gone for a walk but she said she'll watch us.

HILARY   What about Nial?

NIAMH   Are you joking?

HILARY   He's in the contest, isn't he?

NIAMH   No way, he's too cool for a talent contest.

HILARY   But I heard his band were going in.

NIAMH   From who?

HILARY   Grainne's sister Linda said it.

NIAMH   What would she know?

HILARY   She fancies Nial.

NIAMH   What? How could anyone fancy Nial?

HILARY   I think he's cute.

NIAMH   Oh, give me a break.

HILARY   Ask him to come and mark us.

NIAMH   No.

HILARY   Go on.

NIAMH   No. Anyway, he never comes out of his room. Him and Dad are at loggerheads.

HILARY   What's that?

NIAMH   I don't know, there's just always a row.

Dad says he's a loafer, all he cares about is his stupid music.

HILARY   And he just plays the same song over and over.

NIAMH   I know. I told you that... and last Saturday he wore make-up. Dad freaked and Nial called him a prick!

HILARY   Oh my God, that's serious.

NIAMH   Grounded for three weeks so defo won't be doing the contest.

Mam was in bed two days.

HILARY   Why is she not in bed today?

NIAMH   She feels good today.

HILARY   Right.

God, there he is – starting that song again!

NIAMH   Let's turn ours up.

HILARY   We'll move up to the landing... drive him nuts.

NIAMH   Perfect.

She gathers up their gear and exits.

NIAMH *is now left alone onstage as the door downstage left opens.* FIN *enters.*

FIN	Niamh!
NIAMH	Hi.
FIN	When did you get back?
NIAMH	Just now.
	How come you're still here?
FIN	I wasn't going to just leave, Niamh.
	I wanted to wait for you.
NIAMH	Oh… right.
FIN	Are you okay?… How is your mam?
NIAMH	I don't know.
NIAL	What?
NIAMH	They told me to leave.
FIN	Who told you to leave?
	The doctors?
NIAMH	No.
	Fucking Ciara, Dave… Mam.
FIN	Right.
	They probably just thought you'd be better off here.
NIAMH	No, Fin. They simply wanted me gone.
	Pause.
	NIAMH *sighs.*
	I bet you're glad you stayed for tea.
FIN	It doesn't change anything, Niamh.
NIAMH	What?
FIN	I mean, it doesn't change how I feel about you.

NIAMH	Oh Christ.
FIN	It's… I'm not saying it's not a shock, Niamh.
NIAMH	No.
FIN	But Jesus, what's it been like for you? All that… all your life, well, I can only imagine.
NIAMH	Don't… don't, Fin.
	Don't come near me, please. I can't handle it, I can't handle you, not now.
FIN	No no, but it's a privilege, Niamh.
NIAMH	What?
FIN	That's what I'm trying to say – no, not a privilege that sounds nuts I know – but it's good to know, that's what I'm saying.
NIAMH	What's good to know?
FIN	Well… what happened… with Nial.
NIAMH	Dear God, you're as bad as her, Fin. You'll never know.
FIN	No, I don't mean that, how could I? What I mean is that it's a good thing to know about you, Niamh, about your family, your life.
NIAMH	And why is that?
FIN	Because… because we're close… aren't we? We're close and… Jesus, why does this feel like a test?!
NIAMH	A test?
FIN	No, not a test.
NIAMH	You think this is a test?
FIN	No.
NIAMH	Some kind of Mister and fucking Missus.

FIN	No… look, can we stop this?
	Let's stop this.
	Let's.
	Please.
	Let's have a beer.
NIAMH	I don't want a beer.
FIN	Well, tea then.
	Do you want tea?
	I said I'd make tea for Ruth.
NIAMH	Oh fuck, they're still here?
FIN	Yes.
NIAMH	Where?
FIN	Ruth's inside…

NIAMH *looks at him as if to say 'explain'.*

In the living room, she's lying down.

NIAMH	Oh Jesus, all too much for her, is it?
FIN	She's pretty distressed, Niamh.
NIAMH	Hah! She better get used to it.
FIN	Don't give her a hard time…
NIAMH	Oh wow, she's certainly got on the right side of you, hasn't she?
FIN	For Christ's sake.
NIAMH	Not that I can blame you, she is pretty spectacular…
FIN	Now you're just being ridiculous.
NIAMH	I am not… I'm…
	I'm out of order and I know it, in fact I'm afraid I'm going out of my mind… really.

But I'm sorry. I'll try to stop. You're right... Just get me something, give me something that will shut me up. Beer. Paraffin, whatever comes to hand.

FIN   Right.

Good.

I'll make tea.

NIAMH   Fabulous.

He goes back to the counter.

There is a silence now.

And Nial's in there too, is he?

FIN   He was.

Then he went out.

NIAMH   Out?

FIN   Yeah, I don't know, for a walk... for his head, she said.

NIAMH   And is he back?

FIN   I think so, I heard him upstairs.

NIAMH   Did they have a barney or something?

FIN   I don't know... it's been all a bit... you know, with your ma, the ambulance, my trousers.

NIAMH *sighs.*

She was crying.

NIAMH   Was she.

FIN   So I said I'd make her tea.

NIAMH   Right.

Pause.

What happened to your trousers?

FIN	The sick.
	NIAMH *laughs*.
	Then FIN *laughs*.
NIAMH	Oh, I'm sorry.
FIN	It's a tracksuit... I don't know... Ruth got it.
NIAMH	(*Still laughing*.) Oh, fucking hell.
	Welcome to my world.
	He brings over her tea.
FIN	Maybe we should go to my place?
NIAMH	No, I don't think so.
FIN	Give everyone some space.
NIAMH	No.
	I've to wait for word.
FIN	Why?
NIAMH	Because she's at the bloody hospital, Fin.
FIN	I know, but all the others are here.
NIAMH	No.
FIN	We can phone later –
NIAMH	I've to wait for Mam.
	But maybe you should go.
FIN	Me.
NIAMH	Yes.
FIN	I'm not going.
NIAMH	No.
FIN	No.

He has his arm around her, he kisses her, she lets him. She falls into him.

RUTH *enters*.

RUTH   Nial says he'll have that coffee, Fin, if... Oh, Niamh, sorry, I didn't realise you'd come back!

NIAMH *pulls away from* FIN.

FIN   It's okay, we're just... Niamh's just got back.

NIAMH   Yeah.

RUTH   Oh right, great, sorry.

How is your mum...?

NIAMH   I don't know, I left.

FIN   There were too many at the hospital.

RUTH   Oh, of course.

FIN   But they were seeing her all right... the doctors.

RUTH   Oh, that's good.

FIN   Yeah. Niamh thinks she'll be fine.

RUTH   Oh, that's a relief. The poor woman, she seemed so... well, she seemed really ill.

NIAMH   She did.

RUTH   And how are you, Niamh?

NIAMH   Sorry?

RUTH   How are you?

Look, I feel quite... well... quite responsible for all this.

NIAMH   (*Cutting her off.*) I'm fine.

RUTH   Oh.

NIAMH   I just want to wait for Mam now.

RUTH   Oh, sure.

NIAMH   Have things ready for when she gets back.

RUTH   Of course.

              Silence.

              And will Ciara be with her?

NIAMH   I really don't know, Ruth, I presume so.

RUTH   Yes.

              Silence.

FIN   Why don't you go and have that rest, Ruth, you've
              an early start. I'll bring in your tea like I said.

RUTH   Oh, okay, yes... sure.

              She hovers.

              Then exits.

NIAMH   Fucking hell.

FIN   That's why I think that we should go.

NIAMH   I'm not going anywhere, Fin, not till Mam gets
              back.

FIN   Right. Okay. We'll stay.

NIAMH   No, I'll stay, Fin.

              I don't want you near this.

FIN   I'm okay with it, Niamh.

NIAMH   But I'm not. Please... can't you see? I can just
              about breathe in this, there is no room for anyone,
              anything else – not at the moment. I need to be on
              my own.

FIN   Niamh...

              The door opens and NIAL *comes in.*

NIAL   What's happening with Mam?

NIAMH   (*With sarcasm.*) Oh, hi, Nial.

              I didn't expect you still here.

NIAL	Just tell me are they letting her out tonight?
NIAMH	I don't know.
NIAL	Did she seem okay?
NIAMH	She seemed okay…
	They had to pump her stomach.
FIN	What?
NIAL	Jesus.
NIAMH	Yes. Nice, isn't it.
	And it's not the first time.
NIAL	Christ.
NIAMH	She probably took a shitload with you coming.
FIN	A shitload of what?
	NIAMH *sighs*.
NIAMH	Diazepam, Valium, Lexapro – you name it, Mam takes it.
FIN	Oh… right.
NIAMH	Yes.
NIAL	Fuck, I didn't know it was that bad.
NIAMH	No, well, you wouldn't – would you?
	NIAL *sighs*.
NIAL	What is it you want from me, Niamh?
NIAMH	How about my childhood?
	Or my parents…?
NIAL	I can't change anything.
NIAMH	No?
NIAL	I can't.
	Pause.

We're not staying, me and Ruth, we're going in to town.

NIAMH   Of course you are.

NIAL   Look, I didn't cause this, Niamh!

NIAMH   You didn't what?

NIAL   Tonight. I didn't cause tonight. And I can't be dealing with it – I'm sure Mam will be okay.

NIAMH   Yeah, she'll be okay because me and Ciara will take her home, smooth it out…

NIAL   Well, that's your choice.

NIAMH   My choice? I haven't had a choice since the day you went to prison. Do you ever think about that?

Do you ever think about us? At your exhibitions… or painting your abstract cells in Cork? Do you ever think about me or about Daddy before he died, Nial, and his unending campaign to get you out.

NIAL   There was no campaign…

NIAMH   Yes there was. The man wrote to anyone who could read! He was a fixture at the solicitor's office. And that's what fucking killed him…

NIAL   What?

NIAMH   You heard me…

NIAL   Oh! So I'm responsible for that too, am I?

NIAMH   Yes.

NIAL   Jesus, you've already landed Mam in A&E, is that not enough for you this evening, no?

NIAMH   It wasn't me, it was you and your star bride.

NIAL   I never asked for this, Niamh.

I never asked them for anything... But Ma
wouldn't give up, would she? She never gives
up... always the letters, right through Pat's, even
in London there were always the calls. 'Are you
coming home, son?' – pulling me back.

NIAMH   And wasn't she the fool.

NIAL   Ruth just wanted to visit. That's all. Pay a fucking
          visit or something... I mean, that's normal, isn't it.

NIAMH   Not in this family it isn't.

NIAL   Oh God, why won't you stop.

          (*To* FIN.) Can't you stop her, Fin?

          FIN *looks lost.*

NIAMH   But how can I? How can I now it's started, Nial? I
          mean, where the hell were you? When Mam hit
          the floor. When me and Ciara had to drag
          ourselves through school and when Dad choked
          on the stress of it.

NIAL   They told me to keep the head down.

          That's what they said – the solicitors, Da.

          'Keep the head down, son.' I wasn't in bloody
          Butlins, Niamh, what else could I do?

NIAMH   Say sorry! Say why? Say something, Nial.

NIAL   I had to survive. I had to survive it, Niamh.

NIAMH   And what about us?

NIAL   You weren't locked up.

NIAMH   No. No, we weren't, were we? We weren't spirited
          away. Spared.

NIAL   'Spared'? You think I was spared!

NIAMH   You see, we had to live with it, Nial, live in the
          face of it – every day. We had to watch Hilary's

mother! Watch her walk the drive. For weeks, you know. Clutching a jumper. Hilary's jumper. Clutching it so close to her face – frantic for the smell of her daughter, just the feel of her daughter.

NIAL   I won't hear this.

NIAMH   But why shouldn't you hear it?

FIN   (*Softly.*) Niamh.

NIAMH   Mam's always protected you. She's always protected him, Fin.

She'd knock, did you know that, Nial? Mrs Kelly. She'd knock sometimes and ask us to send Hilary home, send her little girl home – with everyone watching, blaming, and the woman near out of her mind.

NIAL   I'm warning you.

NIAMH   Are you?

NIAL   I've spent fourteen years putting this behind me.

NIAMH   So why are you here?

Just tell me that, Nial. Why is it you come back?

NIAL   Because.

Because it's time for something new – with Ruth, she wants, she thinks... and with Mam... we're just trying something new, Niamh, so don't fuck with us... please.

NIAMH   Don't what!... Jesus.

So it's a new charade, is that it?... Is that what this 'visit' is about. It's not 'Nial's Away' any more, it's 'Nial's New Life'!

NIAL   Please.

NIAMH   It all just spins round you. Classic. Even if I've not had a word in years.

NIAL   Because there's nothing to say.

NIAMH   There's everything to say.

NIAL   It's over, Niamh.

            Won't you let it rest.

            I was just a kid.

NIAMH   So was Hilary.

            And so was I!

            Slight pause.

NIAL   Right. I think I've taken enough.

FIN   Come on, Niamh…

NIAMH   Enough! He's taken nothing, Fin. Art college in
            London, therapy, supportive release… Do you
            think I got any of that?

NIAL   I don't know. I suppose you're right about that
            much. I don't know what it's like for you, Niamh.
            In fact, I don't even know you, because I'm a
            different man now and it's a different life.

NIAMH   Yeah? Well, not for me it isn't.

            *They stare at each other. NIAL looks at FIN who
            is stuck at the counter, speechless.*

NIAL   This is fucking useless.

            He exits.

            There is silence between FIN and NIAMH.

FIN   Are you okay?

            *She lifts her hand to stop anything further from
            him, she is struggling now to stay calm.*

            He remains at the counter.

            I might just get my trousers.

NIAMH   Okay, Fin… you do that.

FIN	I think Ruth just hung them on the stairs.
NIAMH	Did she.
FIN	I think they'd be dry by now.

Pause.

	She rinsed them in the sink, you see, she found some powder somewhere and... she rinsed them.
NIAMH	Great.
FIN	Yeah.

So I'll just get them and I'll be back.

Back in just a tick.

All right?

| NIAMH | All right. |

He hovers. She doesn't look at him. He exits.

There is a shift in lighting again. HILARY *comes in and* NIAMH *watches her.*

Hilary?

HILARY *is fluffing up the ra-ra frills on her skirt.*

Christ, I'd forgotten the skirt.

HILARY	What do you think of the ra-ra.
NIAMH	I just love it.
HILARY	Mammy says if she's time she'll do headbands to match.
NIAMH	That's fantastic.
HILARY	But I'm bored with just practising, Niamh.

I want someone to see our routine.

| NIAMH | Mam will be back soon... |
| HILARY | She's taking ages. |

NIAMH   I'm sorry.

HILARY   I'm asking Nial.

NIAMH   No. He won't want to.

HILARY   Yes, he will. I'll be all flirty.

NIAMH   And what the hell is that?

HILARY   *Flirty*. It makes boys think they're cool.

NIAMH   What?

HILARY   I've seen Grainne's sister Linda do it.

NIAMH   How?

HILARY   First you pretend like you're listening to them.

                Really listening… caring.

NIAMH   What?

HILARY   So I'll listen to Nial's song.

                Say it's fab!

NIAMH   But it's awful.

HILARY   I'll say.

                (*Swinging her hair.*) 'Maaaaaaaaaaaan, your song
                is amazing!'

                That's the way I saw Linda do it.

                (*Again with the hair.*) 'You blow me away!'

                HILARY *is laughing.* NIAMH *smiles too as she
                remembers.*

NIAMH   And what'll I do?

HILARY   You have to say it's 'amaaaaaaaazing' too!

NIAMH   I can't, I'll laugh.

HILARY   Come on.

                We'll knock on his door.

NIAMH   What!…

HILARY   Come on.

             NIAMH watches as HILARY runs offstage.

             She sits down. HILARY runs back onstage, laughing.

             He didn't come out, Niamh, he just grunted.

NIAMH   Pig!

             HILARY starts grunting. She laughs, she's getting higher.

HILARY   Come on.

NIAMH   No!

HILARY   Come on.

             She stands and looks at NIAMH. NIAMH thinks then shouts:

NIAMH   We want the pig to come out, Nial!

             And your room's the sty!

             HILARY laughs.

HILARY   Brilliant. Come on so… I want him to watch us.

NIAMH   But he won't.

HILARY   He will.

NIAMH   Anyway I'm hungry.

HILARY   You're always hungry.

NIAMH   There's chocolate!

HILARY   I don't care, come on, I want to amazzzzze someone.

NIAMH   But it's Nial!

HILARY   Who cares?

	I'll knock on the door and you – don't say anything…
NIAMH	I'll wet myself.
HILARY	You better not, Niamh Lynch. Not in me mother's ra-ra!

NIAMH *laughs*.

Wait outside the door, okay!

NIAMH	Okay.
HILARY	I'll get him interested.
NIAMH	Okay.
HILARY	And stop laughing.
NIAMH	I can't.

HILARY *flicks her hair, she's having a ball and enjoying making* NIAMH *laugh*.

He won't let you in, you know, his room is sacred.

HILARY	Is it now?

'Oh, Nial, I think you're amazzzzzzzzzzing!'

NIAMH *smiles again*.

NIAMH	I'll have to just stay here, Hil, I'll die laughing if you do that.
HILARY	Okay, you listen here at the door and I'll 'flirt'.
NIAMH	(*In the same affected voice*.) Okay!
HILARY	Ready?
NIAMH	Yeah.

HILARY *takes a deep breath*.

HILARY	Now! Not a word.
NIAMH	Not a word!

HILARY *gives her the thumbs-up and exits*.

Lights come back up.

There is the sound of DAVE *and* CIARA, *etc., returning.*

Oh God.

Mam!

She goes to the door downstage left.

(*Calls*.) Ciara!

Is she all right?

We hear DAVE *talking as he helps* TERESA *into the kitchen.*

DAVE   Here we are now, T, take it easy.

NIAMH   Are you all right, Mam?

TERESA   Is Nial here?

NIAMH   Nial? He's... I think he's upstairs –

TERESA   Will you get him for me, Ciara.

CIARA   I will in a minute, let's just get you inside.

TERESA   And Ruth?

NIAMH   I believe she's having a lie-down.

TERESA   Oh, bless her.

            All this fuss, it must have her worn out.

CIARA   I'm sure she's fine, Mam.

            Now you promised you'd go to bed.

TERESA   I will, love, just let me see Nial.

NIAMH   What did they say at the hospital?

TERESA   I'm fine, they said everything is fine.

CIARA   They said you'd to go to bed and rest.

TERESA   And I will, once I see Nial...

NIAL *and* RUTH *come in.*

NIAL   Ma!

TERESA   Ahhh, there you are.

          I'm so sorry about all this, son –

NIAL   Are you all right?

TERESA   And Ruth... what a thing to happen on your first
          evening with us.

RUTH   Oh, it's just good to see you back, Mrs Lynch.

          We were so worried about you.

TERESA   Oh, God love you.

          No need.

          Now we can have a nice cup of tea.

CIARA   Mam!

TERESA   I can have tea, Ciara.

DAVE   She'll be all right with tea, love.

CIARA   Okay...

          Okay.

TERESA   Now sit down, love, please.

          FIN *comes in.*

          Oh!

DAVE   Fin, good man.

FIN   You're back.

TERESA   I am.

FIN   And how do you feel.

NIAMH   She feels fine –

TERESA   Why doesn't everyone sit down.

          Niamh!

NIAMH   I'll make the tea.

TERESA   Good girl.

CIARA   I'll just put your things up.

CIARA exits with TERESA's cardigan, etc.

TERESA   Why not get yourself a beer, Dave.

DAVE   Right... sure.

TERESA   And you.

FIN   Oh, thanks.

TERESA   Yes.

DAVE   Anyone else?

NIAL   No –

RUTH   (*Faintly.*) No –

NIAL   Thanks.

Pause. NIAMH is at the kettle.

DAVE is getting the beer.

FIN stays beside NIAMH.

DAVE   Well, we were no time, were we, lads?

NIAMH   No, no time at all.

DAVE   Sure, you're hardy out, aren't ya, T, the doctor
said it himself.

TERESA   He did. Thank God.

Slight pause.

RUTH   So you're feeling better then?

TERESA   Oh, much better, thank you, Ruth.

It was probably a bit alarmist going to the
hospital, but the girls worry.

DAVE   Well, better safe than sorry.

NIAL   Yeah… yeah.

RUTH   Yes.

TERESA   It was really just an upset tummy.

RUTH   Was it…?

TERESA   Oh yes.

DAVE   Yes.

NIAMH   You might have mixed up your tablets.

            Slight pause.

TERESA   Exactly.

            But I'm just so sorry I destroyed the tea.

RUTH   Oh, please…

NIAL   Don't be worrying –

DAVE   It could happen to a bishop!

TERESA   And the thing is that we were having such a nice time.

            Slight pause.

DAVE   Yes.

TERESA   All the chat and the whole family.

FIN   Yeah.

            NIAMH *looks at him. Then goes to bring over the tea.*

            Will I help you with that?

NIAMH   No.

            She brings it over to the table.

DAVE   And you'll have to make sure you go to bed after that, T, or Ciara will string us up!

TERESA   I will, Dave.

Lovely.

Another short pause, no one is having tea.

Now I just have something important I want to give Nial.

NIAL   What?

TERESA   It's a small gift...

NIAL   I don't need anything, Ma.

TERESA   And I have it all ready, hand me over my handbag, Niamh.

NIAL   I don't need anything.

NIAMH   Sure.

TERESA   It's for you and Ruth.

She takes out the envelope.

I know that there's a lot of expense in getting married.

NIAL   Oh, Mam, please.

TERESA   So I want you to have this.

NIAL *won't take the envelope.*

RUTH   Oh no, we couldn't.

NIAL   I have my own money.

TERESA   But these are your father's savings.

NIAL   Jesus.

TERESA   He'd want you to have them.

NIAL   No.

TERESA   I want you to have them.

DAVE   Sure, why don't yiz sort this all out in the morning, ha?

RUTH   Yes, yes.

DAVE   In the morning would be better.

TERESA   But they'll be gone in the morning, it's an early
           flight.

           As CIARA *returns*.

DAVE   And now here's Ciara, T, she'll want to get you to
           bed.

CIARA   What's that?

TERESA   I want Nial to take his cheque, Ciara.

CIARA   What cheque?

NIAMH   Only Dad's savings!

CIARA   What?

TERESA   It's a wedding present for your brother.

CIARA   What?

NIAL   I don't want it.

DAVE   I think you should leave it till the morning, T.

NIAL   I'm not taking it, Ciara.

TERESA   But why not, love?

NIAL   I don't want it.

TERESA   But you do. You need it more than the girls.

NIAL   Stop it, Ma.

NIAMH   Oh, just take it will you.

RUTH   We can't.

NIAMH   Take the bloody cheque and we can all go to bed.

TERESA   Niamh!

NIAL   I don't want it.

CIARA   (*Under them*.) Christ, I'm tired…

NIAMH   You can put it towards your new life.

RUTH   Please. Please. Stop this. It's a really generous
          gesture, Teresa, really generous but Nial and I are
          doing well, we...

          TERESA *puts the envelope on the table and talks
          right over* RUTH.

TERESA   Your father would want it, Nial.

          And that's my last word on it.

          NIAL *still doesn't take the envelope.*

NIAL   Right. Grand, Ma. Whatever you say but I'm
          going to go now.

TERESA   No, no.

NIAL   I am. I can't take any more of this.

DAVE   Take it easy, will you, Nial.

RUTH   He's right. I'm sorry but I really think it's best if
          we –

TERESA   No. No, you're supposed to stay over.

RUTH   But I think we've... I've caused enough upset.

TERESA   Nonsense.

RUTH   We'll find a hotel.

TERESA   What upset?

RUTH   It's not that we're not grateful.

TERESA   What is she talking about?

NIAL   Please stop this, Ma.

DAVE   It's all right, T.

NIAMH   You're getting all worked up again.

TERESA   But that's what's arranged.

NIAL   And I can't do it, Ma, I can't, Jesus.

	How do you all do it, how do you all keep it going?
TERESA	What 'going'? What are you saying?
RUTH	Thank you, thanks for everything, Mrs Lynch.
TERESA	No. No. You're to stay.
DAVE	Will you take it easy, T.
CIARA	Oh, Mammy.
NIAL	Please, please, Ma, if I don't go, I think I'm finished.
TERESA	But why? I don't understand, son, it's just a gift.
NIAMH	It's all Dad's savings, Mam.
TERESA	And Nial needs it.
NIAL	I don't.
TERESA	I need to give you that cheque.
NIAL	No you don't.
CIARA	And what about us?

What about us, Mam? And the kids?

| TERESA | Sure, you'll be all right, Ciara. |
| NIAMH | Yeah, that's it. |

We'll be all right.

NIAL *now makes to leave*.

| NIAL | I'm sorry. |
| TERESA | No, no, son, you're to take that cheque, that's how I planned it. And you're to stay in this house so that tomorrow, tomorrow, son, you can go off on your honeymoon, to be happy, and to the rest of your life. |

Pause.

NIAL   Jesus.

TERESA   Good man.

DAVE   Good man, Nial, will you just fuckin'…
              cooperate…

TERESA   And I'm sorry about the upset.

DAVE   Yeah, yeah, it's all right, T, everything's all right.

              There is a silence.

TERESA   I shouldn't have eaten, Dave.

DAVE   No.

CIARA   Oh, Mam.

TERESA   It was the tea, you see…

NIAL   Christ.

TERESA   And the tablets, that's what caused the upset.

NIAL   We should never have come.

RUTH   We're sorry.

TERESA   No, don't be sorry.

DAVE   For God's sake, Nial.

TERESA   I'm so happy to have you, aren't I, Ciara, I'm so
              happy to have you back.

NIAL   Happy!… Jesus Christ. Is this happy?

TERESA   It's enough for me.

NIAMH   It's as good as it gets, I can assure you.

NIAL   (*Almost explodes.*) For fuck's sake.

RUTH   Nial.

              She reaches for him, he recoils.

NIAL   Just leave it, Ruth.

DAVE   Jaysus.

NIAL	Can't you see it now? The madness of it.
RUTH	I'm sorry.
NIAL	Stop saying that.
RUTH	I just wanted a normal life.
NIAL	But I thought we had that.
	In Cork, in our flat, Ruth.
	But then you had to come here.
DAVE	Nial…
NIAL	I thought we had a chance.
RUTH	We did.
	We do.
NIAL	No. Not any more.
TERESA	What are you saying?
DAVE	It's all right, T.
CIARA	I can't take much more of this.
NIAL	I warned you. I told you.
RUTH	(*Quietly*.) Sorry.
DAVE	Come on, you're not makin' any sense now, Nial, it's been a long day.
NIAL	We never should have come.
	He goes to exit.
TERESA	What's happening, Ciara?
NIAMH	He's just leaving, Mam… like always.
	This halts NIAL.
CIARA	Oh Jesus.
	When will it stop?

RUTH   Come on, love, don't react.

NIAMH   No, don't react, Nial.

TERESA   What's happening?

DAVE   We're going to call it a day, T.

NIAMH   And don't forget your cheque.

NIAL   Jesus, Niamh.

NIAMH   Well, what do you expect?

NIAL   I didn't ask for this, I didn't ask for anything.

NIAMH   But you know you'll get it all.

                No matter what you do to us, Nial. You'll always
                get it all.

RUTH   Stop, please.

CIARA   Why did you kill her, Nial?

TERESA   Oh Lord, Ciara no.

CIARA   Why did you kill Hilary?

DAVE   Shhhhh, love.

CIARA   No. No, I won't, Dave. I've always wanted to ask.

                And it seems so obvious but, I don't know, it
                never seemed possible.

TERESA   Ciara.

RUTH   Please.

CIARA   I came home one day and you were gone, Nial. No
                explanation, no tears – just gone.

DAVE   Don't do this, love.

CIARA   And then, after months of silence, Dave. This kind
                of crazy shaking silence – we moved everything,
                everything I knew.

                New house, new school, new life.

TERESA   (*Weakly*.) Your father thought it was best.

CIARA   But was it, Mam?

TERESA   You were so young, Ciara.

CIARA   Too young to be told? Told anything?

TERESA   How could you understand?

CIARA   And how could you? How could anyone understand killing Hilary Kelly?

TERESA   Stop it.

RUTH   (*Weakly*.) Stop it.

CIARA   Because I remember her. I remember Hilary and she was a funny girl. She was Niamh's friend and a funny girl and I don't know why you killed her, Nial, and I'd like to know that. After all the whispers! After everything! I'd like to know.

RUTH   Don't answer.

CIARA   And I bet if you were honest, Ruth, so would you.

NIAMH   Because that's really why you're here.

RUTH   No. No, it's not.

NIAL   Jesus.

RUTH   It's not, Nial.

NIAL   She was. She was a funny kid.

TERESA   Don't, love.

NIAL   Always messing. Always playing around the house.

RUTH   No.

NIAL   And I liked her, that's the thing, we all liked her, sure she'd been in and out for years – laughing – herself and Niamh.

A nice kid, part of the furniture, the life and, I
mean, she didn't feature but – whatever it was –
that day – they'd been tormenting me – for hours
– knocking, howling at my music. Being kids.

And then she appeared at my door.

She asked me to play the song for her and she
liked it. I knew she liked it. So she asked for
another one.

So I sang.

NIAMH   Oh God.

NIAL   But that made her laugh and I didn't expect that. I
            didn't expect her to laugh and I told her to stop,
            but she couldn't, she was laughing – you know
            those kind of fits of laughing. I think you can only
            have them when you're a kid and then she got me
            going, got me laughing too, well, on the outside.
            So I took up a pillow.

TERESA   No no, son.

NIAMH   I was supposed to stay at the door.

NIAL   And I was only messing, and she was so tiny on
            the chair and she couldn't stop, she was weak with
            the laughing and I was pushing with the pillow
            and then I thought – what would it be like?

RUTH   (*Quietly.*) You didn't.

NIAL   What if I pushed harder. Could I really do it, could
            I really… and then it's like I'm outside myself and
            I can see the veins in my arms with the strength
            and I'm pushing and she's not laughing and I
            don't stop.

            Pause.

CIARA   But why?

NIAL   I don't know.

	I don't know, Ciara.
	Because I could.
TERESA	No no, son, it was an accident.
NIAL	It wasn't, Mam.
TERESA	A moment of madness.
NIAL	I wanted to see what it was like.
	I've always told the truth about that.
TERESA	No.
NIAL	And it was easy, so easy.
	No one was more surprised than me.
NIAMH	I was supposed to stay at the door.
NIAL	It wasn't your fault, Niamh.
NIAMH	But I fancied a Club Milk. Can you believe that? I knew Mam had some in the press, I heard you singing, it wasn't funny any more so I went off to get my Club Milk.
NIAL	It was something in me.
TERESA	Something I didn't see.
RUTH	But you're not that boy, Nial.
NIAL	Amn't I?
RUTH	You're a man now, a different man.
NIAL	I thought so too.
RUTH	You are.
	You are.
	They are all silent.
NIAL	I'm sorry, Mam.
TERESA	That's what you said.

That day.

Over and over.

NIAL   I'm sorry.

TERESA   And you were like a ghost in the corner –
              crouched and sweating – the poor girl on the chair.

NIAL   I couldn't believe it, Mam! It was so easy... so
              quick.

RUTH   Oh God.

NIAL   I was angry.

TERESA   I know.

NIAL   And frightened.

TERESA   I know.

DAVE   You've got to stop this now.

              You've got to stop, Nial – she's not able.

NIAL   No.

DAVE   It's torture.

NIAL   Okay.

RUTH   We'll go, we'll go now, into the city.

TERESA   But there's no need.

NIAL   Please, Ma.

TERESA   (*Raising her voice*.) There's no need.

              Your place is here, Nial, here with your family.

NIAL   Not any more, Ma, I can't do it any more.

              He exits.

TERESA   But I love you, son.

              RUTH *stands at the door. She looks lost. She exits
              after* NIAL.

There is a silence.

CIARA   We better get you to bed.

TERESA   In a minute, Ciara.

DAVE   Come on, T, you promised.

TERESA   I said, in a minute.

           Another silence.

           TERESA *gathers herself.*

           You need to help Nial get his taxi, Dave.

DAVE   What?

TERESA   He's to go into town, didn't you hear him. The
           flight is early so he needs a hotel.

DAVE   Oh right. Yeah.

TERESA   And he won't know who to ring, he won't know
           where to get a taxi.

DAVE   No.

TERESA   So you give him a hand.

DAVE   Yeah, yeah sure, Teresa.

TERESA   And Niamh's friend can help with the bags.

FIN   Right.

TERESA   I just need a minute here, Dave, and I'll see them
           off.

DAVE   Okay.

TERESA   Good man.

CIARA   Okay, Mam.

DAVE   Okay. Fin.

FIN   Yeah.

           DAVE *and* FIN *exit.*

The three women are silent for a minute. Then
CIARA *starts to clear up the tea things with a*
sigh.

NIAMH   (*To* TERESA.) I don't know how you do that.

TERESA *ignores her.*

After what he just told us.

TERESA   I don't know what you mean, Niamh.

NIAMH   You do, you know exactly what I mean.

TERESA   (*With quiet determination.*) I'm his mother.

NIAMH   So?

TERESA   So I might be useless, Niamh, but I'm his
mother... and yours. And I'm still here, I'll always
be here, I won't abandon you like your father.

CIARA   (*Banging the cup in the sink.*) Daddy died.

TERESA   (*With venom we've never seen from her.*) Daddy
chose to die. Daddy couldn't take it any more.
Another ghost – and I'll never forgive him for
that, for leaving me, leaving you.

NIAMH   Jesus!

TERESA   Now I'm tired. I'm sick and tired of it all, Niamh.

I need some peace.

RUTH *enters. They all fall silent.*

She stands for a moment.

RUTH   The boys are just getting the taxi.

TERESA   Are they...

RUTH   So I just wanted to...

CIARA   Mam's going to bed, Ruth.

TERESA   Yes, yes, I'm tired.

RUTH   Of course, you must be exhausted.

NIAMH   She is.

CIARA   She's exhausted.

RUTH   But I just wanted to…

NIAMH   What?

RUTH   Well, I just wanted to make something clear.

            Clear. Mrs Lynch.

TERESA   And what's that?

RUTH   That Nial and I… well… we're going to be okay.

NIAMH   Terrific.

TERESA   (*With no conviction.*) Of course you are.

RUTH   Yes.

TERESA   Well… that's marvellous.

RUTH   Yes.

CIARA   Now she's going to bed.

RUTH   Yes, of course…

TERESA   I'm going to bed.

            The girls will look after you.

RUTH   It's okay, I'm fine.

            TERESA *stops at the door. She puts her hand to* RUTH*'s face.*

TERESA   I'm sure you'll have a lovely time.

RUTH   Oh.

TERESA   And I'm delighted you came, aren't I, Ciara.

CIARA   Yes.

TERESA   We'll see you on the way back?

RUTH *looks at her, totally confused.*

NIAMH   From Spain.

RUTH   Oh... from Spain.

TERESA   Because I'll be looking forward to those pictures
           of the wedding.

RUTH   Oh.

CIARA   She will.

TERESA   We'll all be looking forward.

           Won't we, love.

CIARA   Yes.

           Come on now, Mam.

TERESA   Goodnight, Ruth.

RUTH   Goodnight, Mrs Lynch.

TERESA   Teresa, please.

           You're family now.

RUTH   Teresa.

NIAMH   Night, Mam.

           I'll bring you up your tea.

TERESA   Good girl, good girl, Niamh. I thank God for you,
           I thank God and your father for my children every
           night.

           She exits with CIARA *assisting her.*

           NIAMH *and* RUTH *are alone.*

NIAMH   She's amazing, isn't she? Mam.

           You see, it's over now. Already.

           It never happened.

RUTH   What never happened?

NIAMH   This. Tonight.

The fuss.

She'll just play it all again.

And hope that you call.

NIAL comes in.

NIAL   The taxi's here, Ruth.

She hesitates. Looks at NIAMH.

Are you ready?

NIAMH   What other way is there?

RUTH has no reply, she exits.

NIAL hesitates. He looks at NIAMH.

NIAL   The taxi's here.

NIAMH   Yeah.

NIAL   It is best to go.

NIAMH   Yeah.

He hesitates again.

NIAL   I am sorry, Niamh, if that helps.

Pause.

NIAMH   I don't know, Nial.

NIAL   No.

But you'll be all right?

NIAMH   I don't know.

NIAL   Try, will you, Niamh, will you try.

NIAMH   I do.

His head drops.

NIAL   I said goodnight to Ma.

NIAMH   Good.

NIAL   I'll see ya.

NIAMH   See ya, Nial.

               He exits.

               She sits, she puts her head in her hands. She is trying to pull herself together.

               FIN *enters.*

               NIAMH *doesn't look at him, he stands at the counter.*

FIN   They're gone.

NIAMH   Yes. They're gone.

               She pours herself a glass of wine.

FIN   What are you going to do?

NIAMH   What?

FIN   I mean tonight? What are you going to do tonight? Do you want to come back to mine?

NIAMH   No.

               Look, I'm sorry, Fin, but no.

FIN   Are you sure?

NIAMH   Yeah, yeah, I'm sure.

FIN   Okay.

NIAMH   I'm just... I don't know, I just think I should stay. I need to stay here.

FIN   Okay.

               Sure.

               But I guess I should go.

NIAMH   Yes, you should go.

FIN	Right… and I'll call you tomorrow.
	No reply.
	Will I call you tomorrow, Niamh?
NIAMH	I don't think so.
	CIARA *enters.*
CIARA	Christ, pour me a glass of that, will you.
NIAMH	Sure.
CIARA	Are you having one, Fin?
FIN	No.
NIAMH	No. Fin's just going.
CIARA	Oh, are you?
FIN	Yeah… yeah. I'm going now, the bike's out this way so…
CIARA	Yeah. Christ… well.
	It was great to meet you.
FIN	Yeah. And you, Ciara.
	I'll see you, Niamh.
	She stands up but doesn't go over to him.
NIAMH	Yeah, see you, Fin.
CIARA	Okay.
	Goodnight!
FIN	Night.
	He exits awkwardly through the back door.
	NIAMH *flops back into her chair.* CIARA *sits next to her.*
	There is a pause.
CIARA	He's a good man, Niamh.

No reply. They both drink their wine.

You suit each other…

Slight pause.

NIAMH   Is Mam asleep?

CIARA   I don't know. Dave came up to her.

NIAMH   Does she want her tea?

CIARA   No.

I gave her water.

NIAMH   Right.

CIARA   It's all she should drink tonight.

NIAMH   Yeah.

She'll be fine, won't she, Ciara?

CIARA   I think so.

NIAMH   What do you think of what she said about Dad?

CIARA   About Dad leaving?

NIAMH   Yeah.

CIARA   She was just upset.

NIAMH   Do you think?

CIARA   Dad did his best.

They both did.

Pause. They drink.

It was Daddy came to get me from Kellys', you know.

NIAMH   From Kellys'?

CIARA   Yeah. Mam used to send me, after Hilary died, don't you remember?

NIAMH   No. You were in Auntie Rita's.

CIARA   After Rita's. Don't you remember? She thought it
            would be nice for the Kellys to have a girl in the
            house, to kind of make up for Hilary, so she'd
            send me down with scones…

            NIAMH *looks at her.*

NIAMH   You're not serious.

CIARA   Or quiche.

NIAMH   To Kellys'!

CIARA   Yeah.

NIAMH   With quiche?!

CIARA   Yeah.

NIAMH   Oh, for fuck's sake…

            *She starts to laugh. They both laugh. Almost
            hysterically.*

            DAVE *comes in.*

DAVE   What are you two laughing at?

NIAMH   Quiche.

DAVE   Now what can be funny about quiche?

            This sets them off even more.

            CIARA *continues, still laughing, but eventually
            her laughter dries up.*

CIARA   I'd sit in that house for hours, Kellys, without a
            word. They'd all kind of move around me like I
            wasn't there and I know I was only eight but I
            knew that they despised me, despised us.

NIAMH   Jesus.

CIARA   Mammy had told me to sit with Mrs Kelly so
            that's what I did. I know I did because it was such
            a crazy time… crazed. Wasn't it? I'd just sit there

with Mrs Kelly… with nothing to say. And then Daddy'd come home from work, and I suppose he'd ask Mam where I was… and he'd come and collect me… after dark.

NIAMH   Christ.

I'm sorry.

I don't remember.

CIARA   I was afraid she'd swap me, you know.

Mam.

Swap me for Hilary.

NIAMH   Oh God.

CIARA   Or to get Nial back.

DAVE   That's all behind you, Ciara.

CIARA   I know it is, Dave.

DAVE   You've got me and the kids and we love you.

CIARA   I know you do.

DAVE   So don't be thinking about all that.

NIAMH   You two should go home.

I'm staying here anyway.

CIARA   But Mam…

NIAMH   I'm here, Ciara.

DAVE   She's right, love.

NIAMH   I'll look after her.

DAVE   Come home.

CIARA   But are you sure, Niamh?

NIAMH   Where else can I go?

CIARA   I could come over in the morning.

DAVE	Exactly, come on, you're knackered, Ciara.
	Come home.
CIARA	Jesus, I'd love to.
NIAMH	Go on.
CIARA	Right, thanks.
DAVE	Fair play to ya, Niamh.
NIAMH	Night.
CIARA	Night, Niamh.
	I might just check her on my way out.
NIAMH	Go on with Dave, Ciara.
	You'll just wake her.
	I'll see you tomorrow.
CIARA	Okay.
	Goodnight.
DAVE	Cheers, Niamh.
NIAMH	Night.
	They exit.
	NIAMH *starts lifting glasses, etc., to the sink.*
TERESA	(*Off.*) Ciara!
NIAMH	No, it's me, Mam.
TERESA	(*Off.*) I thought I heard someone leave.
NIAMH	That was Ciara, herself and Dave went home.
TERESA	(*Off.*) Ahhh, did they, love, and the others…?
NIAMH	Yes, gone too.
TERESA	(*Off.*) Ahh, lovely.
	Are you coming up?

NIAMH   I am.

TERESA   (*Off.*) I took my tablets, Niamh.

NIAMH   That's good, Mam.

TERESA   (*Off.*) And I marked the chart.

           NIAMH *sighs. She stops what she is doing. She walks to the door. Looks back into the kitchen. Then turns off the light and exits.*

           The End.

www.nickhernbooks.co.uk

facebook.com/nickhernbooks

twitter.com/nickhernbooks